How to Suppress Women's Writing

BOOK FORTY-THREE

Louann Atkins Temple Women & Culture Series

Books about women and families, and their changing role in society

How to Suppress Women's Writing

* * *

Joanna Russ

With a new foreword by
JESSA CRISPIN

UNIVERSITY OF TEXAS PRESS ◆ AUSTIN

The Louann Atkins Temple Women & Culture Series is supported by Allison, Doug, Taylor, and Andy Bacon; Margaret, Lawrence, Will, John, and Annie Temple; Larry Temple; The Temple-Inland Foundation; and the National Endowment for the Humanities.

Grateful acknowledgment is made to W. W. Norton and Company for permission to reprint lines from a poem by Adrienne Rich, originally published in her *Poems: Selected and New, 1950–1974*.

Book design by Lindsay Starr
Typesetting by Integrated Composition Systems

Names: Russ, Joanna, 1937–2011, author. | Crispin, Jessa, writer of supplementary textual content.
Title: How to suppress women's writing / Joanna Russ ; with a new foreword by Jessa Crispin.
Description: New edition. | Austin : University of Texas Press, 2018. | Includes bibliographical references and index.
Identifiers: LCCN 2017048972
      ISBN 978-1-4773-1625-2 (pbk. : alk. paper)
      ISBN 978-1-4773-1628-3 (library e-book)
      ISBN 978-1-4773-1629-0 (nonlibrary e-book)
Subjects: LCSH: Women authors, English—History and criticism. | Women authors, American—History and criticism. | Women in literature—History and criticism. | Authorship—Sex differences. | Censorship.
Classification: LCC PN471 .R87 2018 | DDC 809/.89287—dc23
LC record available at https://lccn.loc.gov/2017048972
doi:10.7560/316252

This book is dedicated to my students.

Contents

Foreword

JESSA CRISPIN

I have a vision. The streets of Midtown Manhattan are filled with professors, professional critics, editors, and literary award judges. They are all dressed in their ill-fitting suits—they could afford better tailoring but that, of course, would indicate to their audience that something like beauty is important—yet they are tearing them off to replace them with sackcloth. They are on their knees, they are decorating themselves in ashes.

Slowly they crawl out of their blue glass skyscrapers, their suburban commuter rail stations, their off-campus housing to join the mass. It's not a howl that you hear but a low, unceasing moan. A few, the more dramatic and in need of attention, flog themselves with branches and nylon rope. All of these men, all of these white men, every man who ever told a publishing assistant at a party while pinning her to the wall, "You know I am in an open marriage," every man who ever used the word "histrionic" to describe a woman's memoir or "articulate" to describe a black man's performance or who spent two paragraphs speculating about the body of a trans writer in what was supposed to be a review of their work, every professor who uses Kanye lyrics in a lecture to show he is with it but who teaches an all-white syllabus, every man who has referred to a Brontë or Emily Dickinson or James Baldwin as a "minor" writer: they are all here.

They have come to atone. They have come to ask for absolution. They have been forced into an encounter with their unconscious, they have finally seen the truth of their bias—the need they have had to believe that anyone not of their demographic was a charlatan or a bore—and they have been laid low by this information.

The sidewalks are crowded with all those whom they have dismissed and betrayed: everyone who has been marginalized and written out of the history of literature. They are interested in the spectacle, but skeptical. They have seen this type of performance before, this display of "How could I have been so wrong?," which was then followed up either by a return to previous behavior with slight modifications or an attempt to get laid. But they are transfixed by the sight, and they find themselves disappointed that they are still capable of hope: hope that finally they will be seen for their true selves and not through these men's projections.

When the men finally reach the water, they toss their clothes onto the bonfires that have been burning all night. The stench of burning polyester fills the air. "Forgive us," they cry, as they hand over their positions to the spectators and write letters of resignation. "We didn't realize."

Reading Joanna Russ's *How to Suppress Women's Writing*, I wondered, what the hell is it going to take? For decades we have had these types of critiques; we have had books and lectures and personal essays and statistics and scientific studies about unconscious bias. And yet, still, we have critics like Jonathan Franzen speculating on whether Edith Wharton's physical beauty (or lack of it, according to his assessment of her face and body) affected her writing; we have a literary culture that is still dominated by one small segment of the population; and we have a sense that every significant contribution to the world of letters was made by the heterosexual white man, a sense that is reinforced in the education system, in the history books, and in the visible world.

This complaint wasn't even exactly fresh when Russ wrote her book, which I do not say to diminish her accomplishment. It is always an act of bravery to stand up to say these things and risk being thought of as ungrateful. Your small pile of crumbs can always get smaller. But what is it going to take to break apart these rigidities? Russ's book is a formidable attempt. It is angry without being self-righteous, it is thorough without being exhausting, and it is serious without being devoid of a sense of humor. But it was published over thirty years ago, in 1983, and there's not an enormous difference between the world she describes and the world we inhabit.

Sure, there have been some improvements. The ratios of bylines with regard to sex and race have improved, but that was mostly due to persistent online campaigns of shaming rather than any sort of editorial revelation. The unconscious assumptions that create our expectations for women writers or black writers or gay writers often remain the same. If you look beyond the numbers and into content, you'll see that white men are still the experts—still the objective and universal voice of reason. Black writers are often only asked to write about black issues or urban issues or sports or music. Women are often only asked to write about their feelings or work/life balance or domestic issues. Gay writers are asked to write about identity politics or sexuality. And so on. (But while we are at it, we are still mostly only hearing from white men who *want* to provide the objective and universal voice of reason, not all of the weirdos and gender noncomformists and mystics and those marginalized by something other than sex or race, and I long for their presence in the conversation, too.)

And so I ask, again and again and again, what is it going to take to have a full reconsideration of how literature has been dominated by one small worldview, to see how our ideas of greatness are affected by our own need to see our selves, our gender, our nation as great, and to see radical plurality as this exciting, beautiful thing, and not a threat to your tiny little self?

Russ did not write "like a woman," so it's not clear what to do with her. She did not write about domestic or interior spaces; her writing is neither pretty nor diplomatic. As a nonfiction writer and critic, particularly in both this work and the remarkable *Somebody's Trying to Kill Me and I Think It's My Husband: The Modern Gothic*, she does not simply name the injustice, she goes after the source. She understands how a fragile Self will need to define itself against an Other, and she is wise enough to see this is not an issue of misogyny per se but something that has the potential to infect us all. That need for the Other to be a specific something, so that in reflection the Self can be something better, creates a lens that makes it impossible to see the Other clearly without risking the Self. We can only see and judge art through this lens, unless we stubbornly refuse to.

White women will do this to brown women, the rich will do this to the poor, gay men will do this to lesbians or bisexuals. And of course, if somehow we lived in a matriarchy, women would do this to men. This might seem like a banal observation when you read it, and yet so few have written it down before. This makes Russ a keener critic than someone like Angela Carter, whose work has entered the feminine canon because she had a tendency, despite all her wild glory, to say rather banal things about the male/female dynamic. She lined it up much too neatly with the predator/prey dynamic. Carter writes "like a woman," so we know what to do with her. The only other woman critic I can think of who worked on Russ's complicated level was Brigid Brophy, who has also been very unfairly left to languish in obscurity.

As a novelist and short-story writer, Russ did not simply create hazy gender utopias out of her science fiction space operas,

nor did she write in the way of her male peers like Heinlein, Halde-
man, or Ellison, with their big(ish) dicks in space. In books like
We Who Are About To and *The Female Man*, she used speculation to
question the present, not simply to reframe it, putting her more
on a par with Samuel Delany than more womanly writers like
Marge Piercy or Octavia Butler. She had a remarkable mind, one
that found it easy to see through tropes and lazy, self-satisfied
plotlines to mess with the trouble underneath. In *We Who Are
About To*, she firmly and eruditely reveals stories of survival
against the odds, a theme all demographics are quick to indulge
in unthinkingly, which in her case are not heroic tales of endur-
ance but truly about people who are willing to do any amount of
damage to the world, to others, or to the environment to ensure
their own comfort and safety. This woman works so deeply in
our collective unconscious that it's surprising her work ever saw
the light of day.

It would be nice to think that a nonconforming writer burdened by some sort of designator (woman writer or queer writer
or . . .) wouldn't slide into the cracks of literary history, but of
course this is one of the ways to *Suppress Women's Writing*, as she
outlines in this work. We are all burdened by certain expectations
others have for us, but some are punished for their deviations
more than others.

One way she and other writers like her—writers of all gen-
ders and races and sexualities who refuse to meet their audience's expectations—are punished is to not let their influence be
felt. Russ wrote about this in *How to Suppress* in the context of
Emily Dickinson, who, while she is finally seen as a genius, also
is often seen as some sort of singular creature without prece-
dent or antecedent in American letters. She has no mothers, she
has no daughters. People, and by people I mean critics who are
invested in shoring up male hegemony, do not draw a line from
contemporary poets back to Dickinson because, critics assure

us, "she had no influence on anyone." We read her, yes, but she is not integrated; critics do not place anyone within her tradition. Writers like Dickinson become outliers, then, and are isolated from their own nation's or art form's history. It's rejection dressed up as flattery.

And so it is with Russ. She is mentioned and name-checked from time to time, but she has not been incorporated into the wild world of 1970s and '80s science fiction, or women's writing, or American literature, certainly. We do not see her mothers, we do not see her daughters, because critics don't care to tease them out. (This might seem like a minor complaint—not finding a writer's space—and yet it is not a compliment to treat a writer like she is a changeling, or beamed down from a UFO, or sprung up from the earth fully formed. Writers are influenced—they work within traditions—and if that tradition is dominated in the academy by, let's say, Hawthorne and Hemingway, or Heinlein and Dick, that reinforces the singular importance of these writers, and it tells aspiring writers looking for a tradition to help shape their work to read these and not those. Thus hegemony is reinforced.)

But her influence is felt all the same, mostly in other underappreciated or marginalized voices. Christopher Priest, who uses speculation's interrogative powers in much in the same way as Russ, is clearly in her thrall. It would be hard to see a place for Katherine Dunn's deeply weird *Geek Love* in the conservative 1980s literary scene if Russ hadn't made a little space for it by fighting for publication for years. The most exciting voices in contemporary genre or genre-influenced writing, like Nnedi Okorafor and Sarah Hall, work in her wake.

I came at Russ sideways, through Riot Grrl and AK Press distro and those hideously ugly Grove Press Kathy Acker paperbacks, seeing her name-checked by the punk rock chicks who created their own culture through zines and mix tapes when they failed to see themselves in the wider culture. And so her very legitimate lineage, in my eyes, also includes all those girls who gave themselves purposely bad haircuts, who spent hours copying their manifestos at Kinkos on hot pink paper, who sharpied Sleater-Kinney lyrics onto their jeans, who were really into Livejournal for a while. This unofficial passing down of women's writing from girl to girl, from woman to woman, is something Russ notes here as an antidote to women missing from the academy. If the official history neglects to tell you where you came from, you can always create those pathways yourself.

This book, *How to Suppress Women's Writing*, is familiar, yet strange; it is part of a recognizable genre of writing, yet different. She refuses to come to easy conclusions, she refuses to let her exasperation overtake her thinking, and she refuses to let anyone—anyone—off the hook here. She does not apologize for her serious tone, either. After all, what is art but an expression of how we all live and feel? It is not separate from life, it is not frivolous or decadent, it is an articulation of our souls. And if our souls are sick due to unexamined racism, misogyny, or homophobia, then looking at and criticizing art is another way of looking directly at and diagnosing our souls. Or it can be, in the right hands.

Here is my fear: that if Russ is rediscovered, reshelved, and reintegrated, her work will be mistakenly put among all of the other books by women and other marginalized populations: Here Are My Grievances. (Put her where she belongs, in a space with zero qualifications, Literary Criticism or Essays or just Literature. Spare her the indignity of the subgroup.)

It's popular, now that women are gaining voices and power, for us to refuse to see our own hidden unconscious biases and to distract others from seeing them by pointing out the biases held against us. There is a wider and wider market for this in women's writing, because it does not require any thinking and, as another singular weirdo with no mothers and no daughters, Simone Weil, once put it, "There is nothing more comfortable than not thinking."

White (straight, middle-class, gender-conforming) women are now an established market, and because of that, we are pandered to. And it turns out that women often like the same Self-reinforcement that men do. As women gain entry into the halls of power, which have been occupied and protected by men, they show that they will behave in the ways that their predecessors did. They too will demonize, willfully misunderstand, and compartmentalize all of the Other demographics. You can see it in awards for women's writing (it should not surprise anyone that the powerful elite consistently find the writing of this small sliver of women, the sliver that most closely resembles themselves, to be the "best"), you see it in the way women critics review other people's books, and you even see it in the way women now write about powerful men. They use the same exact tactics Russ outlines in this book. In 2015 a white woman complained about sexism in publishing, a black man responded by complaining about the racism of the white women who work in publishing, and another white woman in the *New Republic* (echoed by other white women across the knee-jerk spectrum) told him to please shut up, sexism is definitely worse.

I am worried that new readers of this book will mostly see themselves as the suppressed and not the suppressors—that they will refuse to see their own unconscious biases and the forms they take, such as turning up their noses at a Caribbean writer, for example, for being too localized and not universal enough, or that they'll refuse to read a queer writer because "it's just not my taste, you know?" I am worried that we're all subdividing into tiny, highly specific demographics, and that I'm only going to be encouraged to read the works of other white, middle-class, heterosexual, spinster, Cancer-sun and Taurus-rising women who come from the rural Midwest but now live in an urban area, because only they can truly understand and speak directly to me. It's a cliché that literature builds empathy. It can help you along in that process, but only if you aggressively work against the impulse to treat literature like a mirror. The first step is to notice that you are doing that.

I think what Joanna Russ was doing was trying to figure out how we can truly encounter one another: how we can cross the line from seeing the individual to seeing a shared humanity. That is a radical project. So I urge you, as a reader, not to look here for your own name, your own gender. Not to let this book be a reinforcement of your own worldview. Not to use it to keep from thinking. We owe Russ a bigger debt than that. We are all her daughters.

How to Suppress Women's Writing

Prologue

GLOTOLOG, n., stand. Intergalactic, current:

Dominant sapients Tau Ceti 8 noted for the practice of *frument*, an art form combining aspects of Terrestrial hog calling, Martian slipping involuntarily upon the ice, and Uranian *drof* (lovingly nurturing the growth of slowly maturing crystals by enfolding them in all eight of one's limbs). *Frument*, an activity highly valued by the Glotolog, is performed (according to official histories of the practice) almost exclusively by the Whelk-finned (or "Pal-Mal") Glotolog. Extra-Glotologgi students of the art have found evidence of considerable contributions made by Crescent-finned, Spotty, or Mottled individuals, but historians of *frument* (who are almost always of the Whelk-finned form) tend to either ignore such efforts or condemn them as mediocre, lacking in structure, of technical interest merely, or, above all, *na poi frumenti* ("lacking in the proper spirit of *frument*"). Without the all-necessary *poi frumenti*, according to one famous Glotologgi critic, *frument* loses its artistic character and becomes "merely a lot of inartistic hollering, all the while belly-whopping about in a meaningless and foolish manner on uncontrollably slippery surfaces" (*Frument Kronologa*, q.v.).

It is a traditional and widely held Glotolog belief that the behavior and outward appearance of the Spotty, Crescent-finned, Spiny, and Mottled Glotolog—as well as their relative non-success at the practice of *frument*—indicate that the central essence (or *nerd*) of these types differs from that of the Whelk-finned Glotolog, whose superior essence (*super-nerd*) enables it to constitute not only the artistic but also the social and economic aristocracy of the planet and thereby to enjoy advantages too numerous and varied to be listed here.

Needless to say, Intergalactic science has found among these typically self-deluded brachiopods only the usual minor differences, reproductive and chromatic, which have little direct bearing on behavior and certainly not the overwhelming importance ascribed to them by the Glotolog.

Thus "Glotologgish" has recently entered Intergalactic slang as a synonym for ridiculous self-deception bolstered by widespread and elaborate social fictions leading to the massive distortion of information. Thus:

Na potukoi natur vi Glotologi ploomp chikparu. ("You claim that your subordinate classes are green by nature, yet once during every diurnal period you immerse them in *chikparu* juice; you are behaving Glotologgishly.")—Aldebaran 4.

Shloi mopush gustu arboretum, li dup ne, voi Glotolog! ("When the female weevil displays unusual competence in climbing the tree, you avert your eyes and claim it is a male weevil; how disgustingly Glotologgish of you!")—Dispar 2.

GLOTOLOG, n., colloq. Intergalactic, current:
Information control without direct censorship.

If certain people are not supposed to have the ability to produce "great" literature, and if this supposition is one of the means used to keep such people in their place, the ideal situation (socially speaking) is one in which such people are prevented from producing any literature at all. But a formal prohibition tends to give the game away—that is, if the peasants are kept illiterate, it will occur to somebody sooner or later that illiteracy absolutely precludes written literature, whether such literature be good or bad; and if significant literature can by definition be produced only in Latin, the custom of not teaching Latin to girls will again, sooner or later, cause somebody to wonder what would happen if the situation were changed. The arguments for this sort of status quo are too circular for comfort. (In fact, such questions were asked over and over again in Europe in recent centuries, and eventually reforms were made.)

In a nominally egalitarian society the ideal situation (socially speaking) is one in which the members of the "wrong" groups have the freedom to engage in literature (or equally significant activities) and yet do not do so, thus proving that they can't. But, alas, give them the least real freedom and they *will* do it. The trick thus becomes to make the freedom as nominal a freedom as possible and then—since some of the so-and-so's will do it anyway—develop various strategies for ignoring, condemning, or belittling the artistic works that result. If properly done, these strategies result in a social situation in which the "wrong" people are (supposedly) free to commit literature, art, or whatever, but very few do, and those who do (it seems) do it badly, so we can all go home to lunch.

The methods indicated above are varied, but tend to occur in certain key areas: informal prohibitions (including discouragement and the inaccessibility of materials and training), denying the authorship of the work in question (this ploy ranges from simple misattribution to psychological subtleties that make the head spin), belittlement of the work itself in various ways, isolation of the work from the tradition to which it belongs and its consequent presentation as anomalous, assertions that the work indicates the author's bad character and hence is of primarily scandalous interest or ought not to have been done at all (this did not end with the nineteenth century), and simply ignoring the works, the workers, and the whole tradition, the most commonly employed technique and the hardest to combat.

What follows is not intended as a history. Rather, it's a sketch of an analytic tool: patterns in the suppression of women's writing.

1.
Prohibitions

I N CONSIDERING LITERATURE written by women during the last few centuries in Europe and the United States (I'm going to concentrate on literature in English, with some examples drawn from other literature and from painting), we don't find the absolute prohibition on the writing of women *qua* women that has (for example) buried so much of the poetic and rhetorical tradition of black slave America, although many of the same devices are used to trivialize the latter when it does get written down; James Baldwin's "long line of great poets, some of the greatest poets since Homer"[1] can be easily dealt with by a majority culture in which what is written down is what counts. The fragments that remain are dealt with largely by simply ignoring them, though when such things do surface, more sophisticated methods—to be discussed below—come into play. (For example, education was at first against the law. Then, after emancipation, it became rare, inferior, and unfunded. Such is progress.)

But some white women, and black women, and black men, and other people of color too, have actually acquired the nasty habit of putting the stuff on paper, and some of it gets printed, and printed material, especially books, gets into bookstores, into people's hands, into libraries, sometimes even into university curricula.

What do we do then?

First of all, it's important to realize that the absence of formal prohibitions against committing art does not preclude the presence of powerful, informal ones. For example, poverty and lack of leisure are certainly powerful deterrents to art: most nineteenth-century British factory workers, enduring a fourteen-hour day, were unlikely to spend a lifetime in rigorously perfecting the sonnet. (Of course, when working-class literature does appear—and it did and continues to do so—it can be dealt with by the same methods used against women's art. Obviously the two categories overlap.) It's commonly supposed that poverty and lack of leisure did not hamper middle-class persons during the last century, but indeed they did—when these persons were middle-class women. It might be more accurate to call these women attached to middle-class men, for by their own independent economic exertions few middle-class women could keep themselves in the middle class; if actresses or singers, they became improper persons (I will deal with this later), and, if married, they could own nothing in England during most of the century (1882 was the year of the codification of the Married Woman's Property Act). The best an unmarried lady could manage was a governess-ship, that anomalous social position somewhere between gentlewoman and servant. Here is a Miss Weeton in 1811, who, rescued from oblivion by Virginia Woolf in *Three Guineas*, "*burned to learn Latin, French, the Arts, the Sciences, anything*"—*a desire perhaps exacerbated by her duties as governess, which included sewing and washing dishes as well as teaching.*[2] Thirty years later we find the author of *Jane Eyre paid twenty pounds a year, "five times the price of laundering a governess' not very extensive wardrobe" (four pounds a year was deducted for washing) and "about eleven times as much as the price of Jane Eyre," according to Ellen Moers in Literary Women.*[3] According to M. Jeanne Peterson, Mrs. Sewell, writing in 1865, equated the salary of a nursery governess with that of a lady's maid, that of an informed but not accomplished governess with that of a footman, and that of a highly educated governess with that of a coachman or butler.[4] Emily Dickinson had no money: she had to ask her father for stamps and for money to buy books. As Woolf puts it in *A Room of One's Own, "all those good novels, Villette, Emma, Wuthering Heights, Middlemarch"* were written "by women so poor that they could not afford to buy more than a few quires of paper at a time upon which to write."[5] As for the leisure that, one would suppose, attended this odd kind of poverty, Emily Dickinson seems to have had it (although she participated in the family housekeeping and nursed her mother during the latter's last illness), but according to biographer Gordon Haight the time of the famous Marian Evans (later to become George Eliot) was demanded, through her late twenties, for managing the household and caring for her dying father, she "nursing him night and day . . . looks like a ghost." In 1859, after ten years in lodgings, the famous novelist and George Henry Lewes bought a house; hers were "the responsibilities of housekeeping—buying furniture . . . finding and managing a servant, ordering meals—a task which Lewes sometimes undertook to leave her free to work."[6] Marie Curie's biographer, her daughter Eve, describes her mother's cleaning, shopping, cooking, and child care, all unshared by Pierre Curie and all added to a full working day during Madame Curie's early domestic years, which were also the beginnings of her scientific career.[7]

Nor does the situation change much in the twentieth century. Sylvia Plath, rising at five in the morning to write, was—as far as her meager work-time went—fortunate compared to Tillie Olsen, a working-class woman, who describes the triple load of family, writing, and full-time outside job necessary for family survival. Olsen writes:

> When the youngest of our four was in school . . . the world of my job . . . and the writing, which I was somehow able to carry around within me, through work, through home. Time on the bus, even when I had to stand . . . the stolen moments at work . . . the deep night after the household tasks were done. . . . There came a time when this triple life was no longer possible. The fifteen hours of daily realities became too much distraction for the writing. I lost craziness of endurance. . . . Always roused by the writing, always denied. . . . My work died.[8]

Olsen also quotes Katherine Mansfield:

> The house seems to take up so much time. . . . So often this week you and Gordon have been talking while I washed dishes. . . . And after you have gone I walk about with a mind full of ghosts of saucepans and primus stoves. . . . And you [John Middleton Murry] calling, what ever I am doing, writing, "Tig, isn't there going to be tea? It's five o'clock."

Mansfield continues, blaming herself ("I loathe myself today") and asks for Murry to say, "I understand."[9] (She does not ask for help.)

It is also Olsen, in her heartbreaking biography of Rebecca Harding Davis (in Davis's *Life in the Iron Mills*),[10] who studies, detail by detail, the impossibility of being artist, full-time housekeeper and mother, and full-time family breadwinner. In 1881, Davis writes her son, Richard Harding Davis, "Not inspiration, practice. A lasting, real success takes time and patient, steady work" (p. 149). But she herself, as Olsen makes clear, did not, and could not, take her own advice: "Often there were only exhausted tag-ends of herself in tag-ends of time left over after the house, Clarke [her husband], the babies, for a book that demanded all her powers, all her concentration. Sometimes she had to send off great chunks unread, unworked, to meet the inexorable monthly deadline" (p. 129). It is perhaps no accident that George Eliot, the Brontës, and Christina Rossetti were childless, and Elizabeth Barrett effectively so (one child, late in life, and servants), or that Davis

> ... accepted unquestioningly that ... it was Clarke as a man who should be enabled to do his best work, while her ordained situation as a woman was to help him toward that end: to be responsible for house, children, the proper atmosphere for his concentration and relaxation. (p. 138)

A contemporary writer, Kate Wilhelm, says this:

> ... there were so many pressures to force me into giving up writing again, to become mother, housewife, etc.... My husband was sympathetic and wanted me to write, but seemed powerless.... I realized the world, everyone in it practically, will give more and more responsibility to any woman who will continue to accept it. And when the other responsibilities are too great, her responsibility to herself must go. Or she has to take a thoroughly selfish position and refuse the world, and then accept whatever guilt there is.
> Unless a woman knows she is another Virginia Woolf or Jane Austen, how can she say no ...? It is generally expected

that the children, the house, school functions, husband's needs, yard, etc. all come first. . . . to reverse that order . . . is hard. Nothing in our background has prepared us for this role.[11]

If time is vital, so is the accessibility of materials and training. This may not seem as much of a factor for writers as it does for painters, but if women have never been denied the possession of grade-A bond paper and lead pencils, that may be only because such a prohibition would be impossible to enforce. The history of debarring women from higher education is too well known to need repeating here. What may not be generally known is that the debarring, in modified form, sometimes continues. For example, when I entered Cornell University's College of Arts and Sciences in 1953 I entered (unknowingly) under a female quota. When I entered the college again as a faculty member in 1967 the quota had been increased to 50 percent, and when I left in 1973 the college was in the midst of a battle over whether to abolish the quota altogether and, for the first time in history, to allow female entering students to outnumber male (since the girls competing for places in the freshman class had better academic qualifications, by and large, than the boys).

Certainly in fields where access to materials and training could be controlled, they were. As Karen Petersen and J. J. Wilson point out in *Women Artists*, the two female founders of the Royal Academy in England (Mary Moser and Angelica Kauffmann) are not present in person in John Zoffany's group portrait of the academy's founders, *The Academicians Studying the Naked Model*, but are there "only in portraits on the wall, as they were forbidden by law and custom to be in the studio with a nude figure, male or female." (No other women were allowed into the academy until 1922.) We find, in the next century, that although women could study from plaster casts of the antique, in 1848 "the nude statuary gallery of the Pennsylvania Academy of Fine Arts was open to women only between ten and eleven on Mondays, Wednesdays, and Fridays." By 1883 in the Pennsylvania Academy of Fine Arts, Thomas Eakins' "Ladies Modeling Class," "forbidden access to nude human models," studied anatomy from a cow.[12]

But even though paper and pencil are easier to obtain than canvas and paint, even if one can deal with the matter of time and all the familial obligations that are assumed to come first, even if formal education is not formally denied, there is still that powerful intangible known as climate of expectation. Here in 1661 is Anne Finch, Countess of Winchilsea, blessed with leisure, wealth, and (according to Virginia Woolf) an understanding husband:

> Alas! a woman that attempts the pen
> Such a presumptuous creature is esteemed,
> That fault can by no virtue be redeemed.

And here is Dorothy Osborne's comment on Winchilsea's contemporary, Margaret Cavendish, Duchess of Newcastle, also leisured, wealthy, and "married to the best of husbands": "Sure the poore woman is a little distracted, shee could never bee soe rediculous else as to venture at writing book's and in verse too, if I should not sleep this fortnight I should not come to that."[13]

In 1837 Charlotte Brontë wrote the then poet laureate, Robert Southey, asking his opinion of her poetry. Southey answered "that it showed talent" but "advised her to give up thoughts of becoming a poet": "Literature cannot be the business of a woman's life and ought not to be. The more she is engaged in her proper duties, the less leisure will she have for it, even as . . . recreation." Brontë replied:

I carefully avoid any appearance of pre-occupation and eccentricity. . . . I have endeavored not only attentively to observe the duties a woman ought to fulfill but to feel deeply interested in them. I don't always succeed, for sometimes when I'm teaching or sewing I would rather be reading or writing; but I try to deny myself.[14]

Somewhat later Ellen Glasgow took the manuscript of her first novel to New York City to a "literary advisor" (that is, agent) who told her, "You are too pretty to be a novelist. Is your figure as lovely in the altogether as it is in your clothes?" He then attempted to rape her, letting her go "only after I had promised to come again, and he had kept not only the manuscript but [my] fifty dollars. . . . I was bruised, I was trembling with anger." A publisher to whom she then took her manuscript made no such assault; instead "he wanted no more writing from women, especially from women young enough to have babies. . . . 'The best advice I can give you . . . is to stop writing and go back to the South and have some babies. . . . The greatest woman is not the woman who has written the finest book but . . . the woman who has had the finest babies.'"[15]

In 1881 Leslie Stephen, the father of Virginia Woolf, wrote of George Eliot that she had "a certain *feminine incapacity* for drawing really masculine heroes"[16] (italics mine). Virginia Woolf's husband, Leonard, married to a literary artist and extremely supportive of her and her work, could nonetheless remark to Modern Language Association past president Florence Howe, when she was past thirty, "Why does a pretty girl like you want to waste her life in a library?"[17]

The discouragement is a part of a general discouragement of female learning that is still prevalent; it's not surprising, therefore, to find a twenty-two-year-old student of Florence Howe returning to college after previously dropping out without either of her actions making "a ripple in the family's life." They only had "discussions about whether she really ought to return . . . it would be a waste of money." The same family "greeted her brother's dropping out with alarm" and "had given a huge party" to celebrate his reentry. Howe adds, "diverse stories reported . . . the education of women was . . . unimportant compared to the education of men."[18] Elizabeth Pochoda found the same message conveyed to her even after she got into a prestigious women's college; she remarks, apropos of the students' embarrassment at and fear of dedicated and original female thinkers like Suzanne Langer:

> sexual privacy was . . . above all a persistent reminder of the unreality of intellectual pursuits. . . . these were borrowed robes, and only a fool would wear them beyond the confines of the theatre.[19]

Here are statements collected by women graduate students in sociology at the University of Chicago in 1969 from some of their professors:

"Any girl who gets this far has got to be a kook."

"The admissions committee didn't do their job. There is not one good looking girl in the entering class."

"They've been sending me too many women advisees. I've got to do something about that."

"We expect women who come here to be competent, good students; but we don't expect them to be brilliant or original."

"I know you're competent and your thesis advisor knows you're competent. The question in our minds is *are you really serious* about what you're doing?" This was said to a young woman who had already spent five years and over $10,000 getting to that point in her Ph.D. program.[20]

Discouragement usually takes less obvious forms; I remember a writing student weeping in my office not because her family opposed her writing but because they thought it would keep her busy until she got married: "Nobody takes it *seriously!*" (including an all-male writing class that laughed at her for writing a "Hermann Hesse story"—her words—with a female protagonist). A contemporary of mine, who has now published two novels, said bitterly that her father was more impressed by her hobby of macramé (which "takes the brains of a flatworm") than by her first book. And here is Kate Wilhelm again:

> the family . . . [will] think it's cute or precocious, or at least, not dangerous, when a woman starts to write stories. . . . What I got from my in-laws was that line that it didn't hurt anything, kept me home nights, and didn't cost anyone anything. . . . no one . . . thought it was anything but a passing fancy. . . . It's the condescension that's hardest to take. . . . My first husband never read a word I wrote until after I left him. He knew it was all trivial.[21]

Editors may tell female authors to whom they owe money "that I should ask my husband for more," as contemporary novelist Quinn Yarbro reports,[22] or ask them (as Phyllis Chesler was asked) what they want to spend it on.[23] Or house guests may interrupt a wife's writing as a matter of course (Yarbro again— "He is growing angry because I am putting this before him")[24] while the husband completes the artwork the guest has commissioned. J. J. Wilson comments not only on the expectations surrounding the painter Carrington during her lifetime but on those still held by modern critics:

> . . . an atmosphere of expectation prevailed around him [Lytton Strachey]. . . . everything was arranged so that the future

great man could produce. . . . No one seems to have these sorts of expectations for you, Carrington; indeed all the expectations still seem to be that if you could just have gotten your sex life straightened out, you'd have been fine. . . . in a *ménage* where Lytton Strachey was accepted by all as The Creator, where Ralph Partridge's difficulties in finding a suitable career absorbed everyone's energies, a kind of credibility gap grew up around your image of yourself as a painter.[25]

Sometimes the message that women cannot or should not be artists is very open; indeed it takes the form of advice from the specialists who treat problems in living. Anaïs Nin was told by her psychoanalyst, Otto Rank: "When the neurotic woman gets cured, she becomes a woman. When the neurotic man becomes cured, he becomes an artist. . . . To create it is necessary to destroy. Woman cannot destroy."[26] A later (also male) analyst had to work hard to counter the destructiveness of this advice.

One would like to think such "expert" advice vanished decades ago. But here is Yarbro talking about her adolescence:

Going to a shrink . . . in 1959, when all us females were going to get married and live in the suburbs. Because I didn't expect to (two years on crutches . . . You don't get dates on crutches) . . . and because I was actually planning a career in high school. . . . the shrink told me that I was denying my femininity . . . and that I was envying the male penis, what I needed to do was get laid and pregnant and I'd be fine.[27]

Perhaps most daunting of all is the discovery that the same message can be conveyed by the very high culture to which the neophyte artist aspires. Novelists' female characters, like painters' female nudes, can discourage. Lee R. Edwards, a contemporary scholar, recalling her college education, says flatly:

"...since [no] women whose acquaintance I had made in fiction had much to do with the life I led or wanted to lead, I was not female.... if Molly Bloom was a woman, what was I? A mutant or a dinosaur."[28]

And here is Adrienne Rich:

> all those poems about women, written by men: it seemed to be a given that men wrote poems and women ... inhabited them. These women were almost always beautiful, but threatened with the loss of beauty, the loss of youth.... Or they were beautiful and died young, like Lucy and Lenore. Or...cruel...and the poem reproached her because she had refused to become a luxury for the poet.... the girl or woman who tries to write ... is peculiarly susceptible to language. She goes to poetry or fiction looking for *her* way of being in the world.... she is looking eagerly for guides, maps, possibilities; and over and over ... she comes up against something that negates everything she is about.... She finds a terror and a dream ... La Belle Dame Sans Merci ... but precisely what she does not find is that absorbed, drudging, puzzled, sometimes inspiring creature, herself.[29]

Cultural messages can obliterate even the concrete evidence of female experience recorded by female artists and do so very young. Novelist Samuel Delany reports a conversation with a twelve-year-old who "had devoured all six books of Jean Rhys; she is a pretty bright kid!"

> Me: What kind of books do you like?
> Livy: Oh, well ... you know. Books about people.
> Me: Can you think of any women characters in the books you read that you particularly like?
> Livy: Oh, I never read books about women!

The tragic point is that even a twelve-year-old already knows that women are not people.[30]

One especially lethal form of discouragement occurs when the injunction to be not-a-creator not only saps time, energy, and self-confidence, but is built so thoroughly into the woman's expectations of herself as to constitute a genuine split in identity. Critic and poet Suzanne Juhasz finds Sylvia Plath suffering the split in extreme form: "the exaggerated nature of her suffering . . . resulted from . . . [living in] the fifties, New England, the middle class." Juhasz continues:

There is . . . no need to take sides in the debate that often occurs between the pretty girls and the smart girls as to who had it worse. They both did. . . . for the bright young woman, and especially in American high schools of the fifties, there was only one way to validate the possession of an intellect, by proving that one was as . . . "normal" as everyone else (for normal meant, of course, pretty and popular).

Juhasz adds: "She needed to be good at everything because in that way she could *be* everything: woman and poet." In short, Plath needed to be perfect, but (like every human being) could not be. One way to be perfect remained: "There was perfection in death."[31] So we have:

The woman is perfected.
Her dead
Body wears the smile of accomplishment . . .[32]

and Plath's suicide at the age of thirty-one.

Adrienne Rich speaks of her college years and "the split I even then experienced between the girl who wrote poems, who defined herself in writing poems, and the girl who was to define herself by her relationships with men."[33]

Anne Sexton appears to have felt the same kind of conflict of identity; in 1968 she said in an interview in *The Paris Review*:

> All I wanted was . . . to be married, to have children. I thought the nightmares, the visions, would go away if there were enough love to put them down. I was trying my damnedest to lead a conventional life, for that was how I was brought up, and it was what my husband wanted of me. . . . The surface cracked when I was about twenty-eight. I had a psychotic break and tried to kill myself.[34]

Six years after the interview she tried again—and this time she succeeded. Discouragement can hardly go any further.

2.
Bad Faith

Y ET THEY WRITE. The "wrong" groups (sex, color, class) sometimes work, weasel, sweat, sneak, and audacify themselves past all the informal prohibitions to create a "right" value, i.e., art.

Once the informal prohibitions have failed to work, what can be done to bury the art, to explain it away, ignore it, downgrade it, in short make it vanish?

Whatever these techniques will be, they will have one thing in common: they will be logically fallacious. And their fallaciousness—indeed, often their sheer idiocy—leads to a major problem in trying to talk about them, i.e., how can people actually believe such stuff? Here is Abraham Maslow's view:

> One who has already been put into a rubric tends very strongly to be kept there, because any behavior that contradicts the . . . rubric can be regarded simply as an exception that need not be taken seriously. . . . [In this we find] an

answer to the age-old problem of how people can contin-
ually believe in a falsehood even when truth stares them in
the face.[1]

But how does the rubric itself get started? And past what
point can "reasonable" people "reasonably" continue to believe
in it? In the case of women writers and other "wrong" groups
practicing art, the techniques of containment, belittlement, and
sheer denial are sometimes so very illogical (and so very prevalent) that it's hard not to believe there's a conscious conspiracy
going on—how could anyone argue so idiotically and not be
aware of it? Yet it's equally easy to insist that silliness like that
must be a matter of ignorance—how could anyone aware of
such idiocy not stop, if for no other reason than sheer embarrassment? And if the theory of conscious conspiracy won't do
(with some exceptions, chiefly where money is involved), while
the theory of total ignorance won't do either, what's going on?
(There is a third theory, in which each supposed case of sexism,
racism, or class disadvantage becomes a matter of personal
enmity *here* or chance *there* or some other motive somewhere
else. Such a theory is part of the problem, not its explanation. It
amounts simply to the denial that there is a problem.)
    Conscious, conspiratorial guilt? Hardly. Privileged groups,
like everyone else, want to think well of themselves and to believe
that they are acting generously and justly. Conscious conspiracy
would either quickly stop, or it would degenerate into the kind
of unpleasant, armed, cold war with which white South Africa
must live. Genuine ignorance? Certainly that is sometimes the
case. But talk about sexism or racism must distinguish between
the sins of commission of the real, active misogynist or bigot
and the vague, half-conscious sins of omission of the decent,
ordinary, even good-hearted people, which sins the context of
institutionalized sexism and racism makes all too easy.

I hesitate to mention this social dimension of sexism, racism, and class since it can be so easily used as an escape hatch by those too tired, too annoyed, too harried, or too comfortable to want to change. But it is true that although people are responsible for their actions, they are not responsible for the social context in which they must act or the social resources available to them. All of us must perforce accept large chunks of our culture readymade; there is not enough energy and time to do otherwise. Even so, the results of such nonthought can be appalling. At the level of high culture with which this book is concerned, active bigotry is probably fairly rare. *It is also hardly ever necessary,* since the social context is so far from neutral. To act in a way that is both sexist and racist, to maintain one's class privilege, it is only necessary to act in the customary, ordinary, usual, even polite manner.

Nonetheless I doubt that any of us who does so is totally without the knowledge that something is wrong. To slide into decisions without allowing oneself to realize that one's making any, to feel dimly that one is enjoying advantages without trying to become clearly aware of what these advantages are (and who hasn't got them), to accept mystifications because they're customary and comfortable, cooking one's mental books to congratulate oneself on traditional behavior as if it were actively moral behavior, to know that one doesn't know, to prefer not to know, to defend one's status as already knowing with half-sincere, half-selfish passion as "objectivity"—this great, fuzzy area of human ingenuity is what Jean-Paul Sartre calls *bad faith.* When spelled out, the techniques used to maintain bad faith look morally atrocious and appallingly silly. That is because they *are* morally atrocious and appallingly silly. But this only shows when one spells them out, i.e., becomes aware of them. Hence this one effort among many to do just that, O Glotolog!

3.
Denial of Agency

W HAT TO DO when a woman has written something? The first line of defense is to deny that she
wrote it. Since women cannot write, someone else
(a man) must have written it. Margaret Cavendish,
the Duchess of Newcastle, says Virginia Woolf
was accused of hiring a male scholar to write her works

because she used learned terms and "wrote of many matters
outside her ken." She flew to her husband for help, and he
answered that the Duchess "had never conversed with any
professed scholar in learning except her brother and myself."
[The Duchess adds] She had only seen Des Cartes and Hobbes,
not questioned them; she did indeed ask Mr. Hobbes to din-
ner, but he could not come.[1]

Woolf calls the above "the usual objections," and indeed across the channel a century later Elisabeth Vigée-Lebrun also had to face "the same accusation." In her words:

> One tale was that my works were not done by myself; M. Menageot painted my pictures and even my portraits although so many people could naturally bear witness to the contrary; this absurd report did not cease till I had been received at the Royal Academy of Painting [in 1783].

Fifty-three years earlier, according to Petersen and Wilson, Margareta Havermann had arrived in Paris in 1720 and been accepted as a member of the academy. Then "some doubt arose as to the authenticity of her work," which was attributed to her teacher, not herself. Havermann (unlike Lebrun) was ejected from the academy, "and because of this scandal it was declared that no more women would ever be accepted into the Academy." Adelaide Labille-Guiard dealt with the same charge in Vigée-Lebrun's time by "inviting each member of the Academy jury to her studio where she painted their portraits, before their very eyes."[2]

In painting, although disproof of "the usual objections" is easier, so is misattribution. In the last few years reattributions have begun to occur: the Franz Hals that is really a Judith Leyster, the Jacques-Louis David that is possibly a Marie-Louise Charpentier (but certainly not a David), and so on. Motives seem to have been largely economic—but what of poor Giovanna, who languished glumly in the catalogues for more than three centuries as Giovanni?[3]

Even in literature reattribution theories persist: as late as the 1930s Stella Gibbons could parody male insistence that Branwell Brontë was the real author of his sisters' works (in the character of Mr. Mybug, the Lawrentian nitwit of her Cold Comfort Farm) and link such theories to the male chauvinism and personal vanity of the theorizer.[4]

But there are subtler alternatives to the flat denial of agency: *She didn't write it; he did.* One is: *It wrote itself.* This is highly unlikely, and yet the ploy is used, and not only in the nineteenth century. For example, Percy Edwin Whipple, reviewing *Jane Eyre* in *the North American Review* of 1848, supposed that two persons had written it, a brother and sister, since: "... there are niceties of thought and emotion in a woman's mind which ... often *escape unawares* from a female writer"[5] (italics mine). Or, in the twentieth century, about the author of *Frankenstein*, according to Ellen Moers:

> Her extreme youth, as well as her sex, have contributed to the generally held opinion that she was not so much an author in her own right as a transparent medium through which passed the ideas of those around her. "All Mrs. Shelley did," writes Mario Praz, "was to provide a passive reflection of some of the wild fantasies which were living in the air around her."[6]

A much more subtle version of the same thing can be found in Mark Schorer's account of *Wuthering Heights* in 1949, i.e., that the writing of the book did not proceed under the novelist's control, that she began by wishing to write one kind of book and ended by writing another, that the book was a "moral teething" for the novelist and "her metaphors instruct her, and her verbs ... *demand* exhaustion just as [her] metaphors *demand* rest" (italics mine). Carol Ohmann sums up this view of the novel: "the art of composition is figuratively denied to the novelist. Emily Brontë began writing *Wuthering Heights* but it finished itself."[7]

It is almost refreshing to find a nineteenth-century critic whose generous version of *It wrote itself* is merely: *Part of it wrote itself; she wrote the other part.* Thus George Saintsbury in 1895 insists only that George Henry Lewes' "scientific phraseology... invaded his companion's [Eliot's] writing with a positive contagion"[8]— like measles, no doubt—though according to one of George Eliot's biographers she had studied the sciences long before she met Lewes.[9]

Since *It wrote itself* looks pretty silly, even as metaphor, some critics have invented a subtler version that appears to restore agency to the female author while actually insisting that some "he" had to write it, that is: *The man inside her wrote it.* Mary Ellmann characterizes this phenomenon as "the hermaphroditic fallacy according to which one half the person, separating from the other self, produces a book by binary fission. So Mary McCarthy has been complimented . . . on her 'masculine mind.'"[10]

In *Ces Plaisirs* Colette similarly deals with the impossibility of a woman's writing by splitting herself in two. Thus she speaks of herself as "secretly craving... to be *completely* a woman," and of the *"masculine* streak" in her character. She has another character speak of *"masculine* wit" or the *"feminine* streak" in some men. Colette, who wishes to be *"completely and stupidly female"* gazes at a man "with ... *male* wistfulness" (italics mine).[11] Human or personal complexity is reduced to two sets of characteristics, one male, one female. The "stupid" woman who writes does so by using her "masculine wit."

The Jungian theory of anima/animus as used by some modern writers seems to me a prolongation of the same split. Here is a contemporary, Ursula LeGuin, wrestling with a subtler version of her "man's mind":

Male artists have been aware enough of the essential role in their work of their anima . . . the Muse, the Creator Spirit in the feminine gender. . . . In my own experience, the Creator

Spirit is more masculine than feminine, but on the deeper levels is both at once.

I have of course wondered why I write about men more often than about women; possibly because my animus seeks [an] expression . . . it finds limited in the non-writing part of my life, which is seen by my society as "feminine." . . . a single woman or one without children working in the male-oriented job market . . . might . . . reach balance by writing mostly about women.[12]

As for my own experience, in 1972 or thereabouts I was told at a writer's party by a male colleague that I was a wonderful writer who "did not write like a woman" and that—pianistically speaking—I had a man's "reach." Sonya Dorman, a contemporary short story writer and poet, speaking of a story of hers published in 1970, writes:

I just received, in the same mail as your . . . letter, a fan post-card, saying he liked Bye Bye Banana Bird & Heinlein couldn't have done it better.

Godddamn it. HEINLEIN COULDN'T HAVE DONE IT AT ALL.

I am now joining N.O.W., W.O.W, P.O.W., & any other anti-establishment (the Establishment is male, of course) group that'll have me.[13]

In its final, most subtle form, the denial of agency takes the form: A woman did not write this because the woman who wrote it is *more than a woman*. (The highest praise Dickens could bestow on his dead sister-in-law, Mary Hogarth, was that she "was in life almost *as far above* the foibles and vanities of *her sex and age* as she is now in Heaven"[14] (italics mine).

Robert Lowell's admiring foreword to Sylvia Plath's *Ariel* takes a similar view: "Sylvia Plath becomes . . . something imaginary, newly, wildly created—hardly a *person* at all *or a woman*, certainly not a 'poetess'"[15] (italics mine). Who is this "person" who is more than a woman? Some time in 1974 or early 1975 Samuel Delany had lunch in London with a British editor working for a new paperback firm. The conversation, as Delany reports it, went like this:

"Do you know anything of Joanna Russ?" . . . "Ah," he said. "When I was working for _____ [Books], two years ago, I rejected two of her novels—I didn't even get a chance to read them. My boss told me women science fiction writers don't sell." . . .

"Doesn't _____ [Books] publish Ursula LeGuin?" I asked. Next to Heinlein and . . . Asimov, Anderson, Aldiss . . . for the last six months, Ursula has been the widest-distributed science fiction writer in the British Isles.

"Oh, yes. In fact, it's the same editor who told me women science fiction writers didn't sell who bought her books."

"Well . . . maybe the situation has changed. LeGuin is selling very well."

"Oh well, I haven't read LeGuin, but *he's* supposed to be very good." And he then went on to refer to Ursula alternately as "he" and "she" over the next five sentences at least six times.[16] [italics mine]

Ancient methods can be resorted to in a pinch, of course. Quinn Yarbro reports a discussion between two male colleagues of hers about female authors. The first is Vonda McIntyre:

"Well, look . . . she's been running all those workshops. She's had a lot of help." The mystery pro (also male), somewhat taken aback at this, then mentioned Ursula and expressed a great deal of admiration for her. "Yeah," the science fiction pro agreed, "but you know who her father was."[17]

4.
Pollution of Agency

S O SHE DID WRITE IT.
But ought she to have done so?
An alternative to denying female agency in art
is to pollute the agency—that is, to promulgate the
idea that women make themselves ridiculous by
creating art, or that writing or painting is immodest (just as displaying oneself on the stage is immodest) and hence impossible
for any decent woman, or that creating art shows a woman up as
abnormal, neurotic, unpleasant, and hence unlovable. *She wrote
it, all right—but she shouldn't have.*

Thus our poor Duchess of Newcastle, blamed for not having
written her work herself, is also judged mad for having written
it. And Lady Winchilsea imagines her "lines decried" as a "presumptuous fault."

Literary history is, I think, familiar with the Catch-22 by
which women who were virtuous could not know enough

about life to write well, while those who knew enough about life to write well could not be virtuous. The subject of nineteenth-century attitudes on the matter is well enough known (the whole matter of preventing women painters studying from the nude—even the nude bodies of other women—is clearly an attitude of this sort), but it might be worth noting that as late as 1892, according to Virginia Woolf, who deplored such restriction,

> Gertrude Bell "went with Lizzie, her maid, to picture exhibitions; she was fetched by Lizzie from dinner parties; she went with Lizzie to . . . Whitechapel . . ." (*Three Guineas*, p. 165)

Woolf describes Bell's life further:

> Chastity was invoked to prevent her from studying medicine; from painting in the nude; from reading Shakespeare; from playing in orchestras; from walking down Bond Street alone. . . . In the beginning of the present century the daughter of an ironmaster . . . Sir Hugh Bell, had "reached the age of 27 and married without ever having walked alone down Piccadilly . . ." (p. 168)

The assumption that acting, when women did it, was tantamount to prostitution, persisted astonishingly (and may have vanished only with the advent of the movies, female movie stars having taken over that particular myth of promiscuity). In *Villette*, one of the book's most discouraging exchanges occurs when the heroine, Lucy Snowe, attends a performance given by the tragedienne "Vashti" (modeled on the famous French actress, Rachel). Lucy is impressed by the performance and the tragedienne, whom she compares—in three pages of splendid description—to no less a personage than Lucifer. For example:

Wicked, perhaps, she is, but also she is strong: and her strength has conquered Beauty, has overcome Grace, and bound both at her side. . . . Fallen, insurgent, banished, she remembers the Heaven where she rebelled. . . . Place now the Cleopatra [a nude figure at which, earlier in the novel, Lucy has been forbidden to look at on the grounds of impropriety], or any other slug, before her as an obstacle, and see her cut through the pulpy mass as the Scimitar of Saladin clove the down cushion.

Lucy asks John Bretton, her companion in the theater, and a man she loves, for his opinion of the artist:

I longed to know his exact opinions [*sic*]. . . . "How did he like Vashti?" . . . In a few terse phrases, he told me his opinion of, and feeling towards, the actress: *he judged her as a woman, not an artist*: it was a branding judgment.[1] [italics mine]

Villette was published in 1853. In the 1890s the immorality of actresses was still a popular myth. George Bernard Shaw gleefully describes a newspaper controversy of 1897–1898, in which Clement Scott, interviewed in the journal *Great Thoughts*, had said that "actresses are not, as a rule . . . 'pure,' and their prospects frequently depend on the nature and extent of their compliances." Shaw, retorting that "If an actress has commanding talent, and is indispensable on stage, she can be what she likes," still finds it necessary to make an exception for "their [the stars'] humbler colleagues" in his review of December 25, 1897. In his review of January 22, 1898, he declares, perhaps more in his own element:

The controversy about the morality of the stage has been stabbed stone dead by an epigram. Mr. Buchanan's

"Thousands of virtuous women on the stage and only six actresses!" is irresistible.

Perhaps (one hopes) partly in reaction to his own earlier contribution to their idiocy ("their humbler colleagues"—though Shaw was not at times above characterizing marriage in the same terms as Emma Goldman) he adds: "Our habit of flooding the newspapers with prurient paragraphs about women . . . is not a habit of threshing out moral questions."[2]

Elaine Showalter has documented the fear of impropriety that was ever-present to condemn or hinder women writers in England. Thus:

> Arguments *ad feminam* in periodical reviewing were so characteristic of the years from 1840 to 1870 that I could not begin to list them all. Most of the talented women writers of the period were criticized for "coarseness" or a lack of ladylike refinement. Anne Brontë's . . . *The Tenant of Wildfell Hall* . . . scandalized James Lorimer of *The North British Review* with its "coarseness and brutality." . . . Elizabeth Barrett Browning was called by the *Edinburgh Review* "often . . . more coarsely masculine than any other woman writer." . . . [of *Aurora Leigh*] *The Westminster Review* commented . . . "she takes the wrong means to prove her manhood . . . she . . . becomes coarse . . . she swears without provocation."

Of *Jane Eyre*, "many critics bluntly admitted that they thought the book was a masterpiece if written by a man, shocking or disgusting if written by a woman." Impropriety also spilled over from life to work:

> While she was finishing *The Mill on the Floss*, George Eliot became so anxious and sensitive [due to "possible moral

outrage" at her union with Lewes] that she wrote to Black-
wood's, asking if they wished to remain her publisher, since
her identity became known. [They did.]

Perhaps this pollution of agency explains the increase in masculine pseudonyms among women authors during the last half
of the nineteenth century, at a time when anonymity was being
abandoned in periodical journalism; Showalter lists twelve
examples from the 1850s to the 1880s.[3]

Surely such pollution of agency via impropriety disappeared
with the nineteenth century. And yet here is Louis Simpson's
1967 review of Anne Sexton's *Live or Die*: "A poem entitled 'Menstruation at Forty,' was the straw that broke the camel's back."[4]
More tellingly, perhaps, a modern scholar, Dolores Palomo, reading twentieth-century criticism of eighteenth-century women
novelists, can find: "a sort of literary double standard . . . women
writers are allowed to be cloyingly moralistic but never out-
spoken, libertine, or free thinking." Her example is Mrs. Mary
Manley, politically notorious in her own day (she was jailed
for books that were libels on the Whigs), but notorious in our
own century for novelistic prurience and an abandoned life
which really consisted of two long-term affairs after her husband deserted her. In modern works ranging from a standard
literary history of English to Trevelyan's history of the period
one finds: "scandal . . . unsavory"; "a woman of no character";
"scurrilous and indecent"; "easy virtue"; "scandalous . . . indecency"; "erring matron"; "depravity"—the slurs being equally
distributed between the writer and the works. Yet Swift, who
left "the best known and most comprehensive contemporary
opinion of her, describes her as dropsical, homely, fat, forty, and
'of very generous principles.'"[5]

But (one might argue) although menstruation is considered improper, it is, after all, a small part of women's experience

and men will get used to it; moreover a generation which has made best sellers of Lisa Alther's *Kinflicks* and Erica Jong's *Fear of Flying* no longer attacks female authorship via accusations of impropriety.

Is it possible, then, for women to write about anything?

Not quite.

I believe that pollution of agency has only shifted its ground, that *Fear of Flying* and *Kinflicks* are tolerated because they are sexually (and economically) dishonest, women "talking dirty" in a way that's acceptably cute, just as Lois Gould's *Such Good Friends* is acceptably masochistic, like Joan Didion's passive, depressed heroines whose unhappiness is praised by the author as a sign of special, feminine sensitivity. What remains unacceptable is clearly marked, not by "impropriety" (the nineteenth-century term), but by the modern "confessional." According to critic Julia Penelope [Stanley], this pejorative label combines two ideas: that what has been written is *not art* (a version of the nineteenth-century idea that women write involuntarily) and that such writing is *shameful* and *too personal* (the writer should not have felt or done such things in the first place, and if she had to do such things or feel that way, she certainly should not have told anyone about it). Defending Kate Millett's *Flying* against a female reviewer's charge of "confessional," Penelope argues:

> ... critics would have us believe that "confessional" literature is so personal in its content, so specific in its telling that ... [it has no] value as "literature."

She adds:

> ... characterizing *Flying* as "confessional" can imply that Kate has done something embarrassing and inappropriate for which transgression she is in need of absolution.

Noting that the confessions of Rousseau or St. Augustine, the "ecstatic religious poems of John Donne," and "the 'terrible' sonnets of Gerard Manley Hopkins" are not condemned as "confessional," Penelope concludes that "the distinction between autobiography and confession is only expedient." In short, "the label is simply handy for dismissing art that the critic wishes to trivialize." She quotes Erica Jong: "It's become a put-down term for women, a sexist label for women's poetry."[6]

As Penelope notes, male accounts of intense, autobiographical experience are not usually put down by being called "confessional." I would add that the female art thus labeled is called "confessional" because of the nature of the experience (not simply its femaleness)—Plath's rage, Sexton's madness, and Millett's lesbianism are "confessional" while Didion's acceptable female masochism and the sexual misery of *Kinflicks* (disguised as cheery satire and happy obscenities) are not. Even Lowell's admiring foreword to *Ariel* swerves automatically to the automatic condemnation, if only to deny it: Plath is *not* confessional, hallucinating, or a "poetess." That is, she is not what anyone might reasonably expect her to be:

> Everything in the poems is personal, confessional, felt, *but* the manner of feeling is *controlled* hallucination.[7] [italics mine]

What appears to be at issue here is the same old specter of immorality, with the taboos located in essentially the same places: rage, accusation (or accusatory despair), and unacceptable sexuality.

The taboo on these areas is not new. In 1848 the *Quarterly Review* criticized the tone of *Jane Eyre* as that which "has overthrown authority and violated every code human and divine abroad, and fostered Chartism and rebellion at home."[8] Even George Henry Lewes, the friend and encourager of female novelists, could write of Charlotte Brontë's *Shirley* in a review (about the portrayal of Mrs. Pryor, who abandons her child because it resembled its detested and depraved father):

> "Currer Bell! . . . if ever under your heart had stirred a child, if to your bosom a babe had been pressed,—that mysterious part of your being towards which all the rest of it was drawn, in which your soul was transported and absorbed— never could you have *imagined* such a falsehood as that!" No wonder Charlotte Brontë wrote to him . . . "I can be on guard against my enemies, but God deliver me from my friends."[9]

In 1977 Olga Broumas, Yale Younger Poet, published a volume of poems, entitled *Beginning with O.*[10] Many of the poems were lesbian love poems. The result? Threatening and obscene phone calls from her fellow citizens of Eugene, Oregon. (As of this writing, the voters of Eugene have just repealed laws protecting homosexuals against discrimination in employment and housing.) The tabooed areas remain the same: unacceptable sexuality and rage. Plath's work is "confessional"; Allen Ginsberg's is not. Rage in men may be anything from revolutionary to silly—but in most reviewing it's not "confessional." Clearer examples may be found in painting, an art in which pollution of agency via immodesty is still very active. For example, only very recently have women begun to paint male frontal nudity. In *About Men* Phyllis Chesler reproduces Sylvia Sleigh's "Double Images: Paul Rosano," nude front and back portraits of a young man. Chesler states, "Sleigh has often had difficulty in exhibiting her male nudes. People—men and women—have demonstrated, brought pressure to bear, and upon occasion have had the 'offending' frontally nude canvases removed from public view. . . . Sleigh, unlike da Vinci, Verrocchio, and Michelangelo,

for example, paints her nude men *for women, as* a woman . . .
not . . . for homosexual men, as a homosexual. . . . Her male
nudes . . . appeal to *women's* interest. This, I think, is the source of
her troubles"[11] (italics Chesler's).
A form of pollution allied to immodesty is unlovableness;
this too begins early. Lady Mary Wortley Montagu, writing to her
daughter, Lady Bute, in 1753, warns that Lady Bute's daughter
(Lady Mary's granddaughter) must "conceal whatever learning
she attains with as much solicitude as she would hide crooked-
ness or lameness" since "men have engrossed [fame] to themselves."[12] According to Rousseau:

> A female wit is a scourge to her husband, her children, her
> servants, to everybody. . . . she is always trying to make a
> man of herself. . . . Outside her home she is very rightly a butt
> for criticism. . . . We can always tell what artist or friend
> holds the pen or pencil when they are at work.[13]

Rousseau's all-purpose denunciation adds denial of agency
to abnormality ("trying to make a man of herself"). Stendahl is
kindly rather than denunciatory, but the message is the same:

> a woman must never write anything but posthumous
> works. . . . For a woman under fifty, to get into print is sub-
> mitting her happiness to the most terrible of lotteries; if
> she has the good fortune to have a lover, she'll begin by los-
> ing him.[14]

Ellen Moers, discussing Madame de Stael's tremendously influ-
ential novel, *Corinne,* states that it

> suggests both the glamour and the risk that attends the
> woman who gives herself spiritually and physically to a wide

public, while offending, exciting, and perhaps losing the single lover who awaits her in the privacy that is a romance.[15]

Currently, stereotypes of the female artist as personally unlovable (or unloved) seem to have migrated to the movies—shades of *The Red Shoes!*—while complaints about literary women's unpleasantness have taken a different route. J. M. Ludlow, in a nineteenth-century review of Elizabeth Gaskell's *Ruth*, could call himself no admirer of "women authors as such . . . with ink halfway up their fingers, and dirty shawls, and frowsy hair . . ." but in the nineteenth century, the sheer fact of a woman's being a woman was not, in itself, ludicrous—her inferiority was too serious a matter. So Lewes can attack "Currer Bell" publicly for her scurrility in not considering the mother-child bond sacred and Thomas Moore can, anonymously, in verse, mock Harriet Martineau's "unsexed" barrenness:

Come wed with me . . .
Chas'd from our classic souls shall be
All thoughts of vulgar progeny;
And thou shalt walk through smiling rows
of chubby duodecimos,
While, I, to match thy products nearly,
Shall lie-in of a quarto yearly.[16]

Certainly there is enough written opinion during the nineteenth century (and twentieth) about the inferiority of women. What is striking in the following modern examples, culled from Mary Ellmann's *Thinking about Women*, is the change in tone—from serious lecturing to automatic contempt via feminine stereotypes, from hostility directed at the "wrong" kind of women (childless or improper) to hostility directed (it seems) at all women. One cannot escape the impression, reading

Ellmann's book, that to a great many male critics and writers in recent years, there is something wrong about simply being a woman. One notes, also for the first time, that the preference for masculinity is expressed in directly genital terms. Thus Anthony Burgess, who dislikes Jane Austen's novels, writes: "I can gain no pleasure from serious reading . . . that lacks a strong male thrust . . . a brutal intellectual content" (p. 23). But when Burgess does find intellectual content, he dislikes it; Brigid Brophy's logic is not "lovable" (p. 25). Nor is Burgess pleased with George Eliot: "The male impersonation is wholly successful." Or Ivy Compton-Burnett: "A big sexless . . . force" (p. 40). For some reason, Ms. Brophy comes in for the worst of it in the next few chapters; here is the *Times Literary Supplement* of June 1, 1967: "Brigid Brophy has won herself a small reputation in recent years as one of our leading literary shrews" (p. 137). Perhaps this is because she's pretty: "An American professor of mine, formerly an admirer of Miss Brophy's work, could no longer think of her as an author once he'd seen her in the flesh. '"That girl was made for love,' he would growl" (p. 41). When a critic wishes to refer scathingly to Simone de Beauvoir, the phrase is "the lady" (for her tolerance of de Sade) and then—for her qualifications of that tolerance— she is spoken of as reluctant to "give herself" to de Sade (p. 42). Ellmann emphasizes the brevity and sufficiency of this kind of sexual slur by quoting an argument between Elizabeth Hardwick and Frederick Crews; Crews simply calls Hardwick "hysterical" (p. 84). It is sometimes enough (and, apparently publicly acceptable) simply to describe one's "ideal theater critic"— again briefly and without giving the accompanying Victorian lecture—as Lionel Abel does: "I want a man to go, first of all, not a woman (I do have some prejudices), and I want the man to be stoutly uneffeminate (still more prejudice)" (p. 150). So wrong is it merely to be a woman that the femininity supposed to exist in male homosexuals is equally wrong per se; hence "Flannery

O'Connor is praised not only as a woman writer who writes as well as a man might wish to write, but also as a woman writer who succeeds in being less 'girlish' than Truman Capote or Tennessee Williams" (p. 32). And Richard Gilman, dispraising Philip Roth, consigns him to the "ladies' magazine" level (pp. 38–39). At its worst this kind of criticism becomes the insistence that *women are the enemy* [italics Ellmann's] ... (when the word *enemy* is thrown past Leslie Fiedler, he immediately returns, like a basset, a description of a middle-aged, middle-class woman who uses her membership in some, any, every organization ... [to harass] liberal imaginations)" (p. 96). At its kindest, "phallic criticism," in Ellmann's words, imposes "an erogenic form upon all aspects of the person's career"; for example, she quotes Stanley Kauffman: "Poor old Françoise Sagan ... her career in America resembles the lifespan of those medieval beauties who flowered at 14, were deflowered at 15, were old at 30 and crones at 40" (p. 30).

I thought Ellmann was exaggerating until three short plays of mine were produced off-off Broadway in 1969, one year after the publication of *Thinking about Women*. The *Village Voice* review, in the main a favorable one, declared the plays to be "like would-be brides, clever in charting their arrangements, tactful and alluring, but never quite making it all the way down the aisle."[17]

And here is Norman Podhoretz, explaining the rapidity of Susan Sontag's rise as a critic:

> the availability of a vacant position in the culture. . . . Dark Lady of American Letters. . . . Miss McCarthy no longer occupied it, . . . having been recently promoted to . . . *Grande Dame*. . . . The next Dark Lady would have to be, like her, clever, learned, good-looking, capable of writing family-type criticism as well as fiction with a strong trace of naughtiness. But . . . by the 1960s, it was not nearly enough to confess to

having slept with The Man in the Brooks Brothers Shirt. . . .
hints of perversions and orgies had to be there. . . . her figure
mystically resembled that of the young Mary McCarthy and
she had the same rich black hair.

Elaine Reuben comments, "a female critic/intellectual is judged
on her figure, her hair, and her ability to talk dirty," and adds the
nervous comment of Elizabeth Hardwick (herself a critic) on
this kind of "erogenic" imposition (as Ellmann calls it):

> A great measure of personal attractiveness and a high degree
> of romantic singularity are necessary to step free of the . . .
> governessy, the threat of earnestness and dryness. . . .
> Madame de Stael . . . needed her rather embarrassing love
> affairs to smooth over, like a cosmetic cream, the shrewd
> image.

Reuben adds: "Hardwick apparently accepts the rule: women
should not only dress to be attractive to men; they must write to
be attractive to them."[18]
     Probably what underlies the assumption of Ellmann's "phal-
lic criticism" that women are ludicrous and dislikable except
in bed—and sometimes even there—or to be judged by wholly
erotic criteria even when they try to act publicly is popularized
Freud, that is, Pollution of Agency via abnormality. (I have not
quoted Norman Mailer, although Ellmann does so frequently;
his is phallic criticism *ad absurdum*.) Nor is the popularized version so far from the original. Rousseau's insistence was that the
female intellectual "is always trying to make a man of herself."
In *Patriarchal Attitudes* Eva Figes traces German anti-feminism,
picking up along the way that eerie caricature of Freudian genital theories, Otto Weininger:

intellectual women . . . have a large proportion of maleness in their makeup. This is why George Sand used a male pseudonym and wore trousers, because "some of the anatomical characteristics of the male" lurked under those velvet pants. . . . He also comments on George Eliot's large, masculine forehead.

Here is Freud himself:

> The wish to get the longed-for penis . . . may contribute to the motives that drive a mature woman to analysis, and what she may reasonably expect from analysis—a capacity, for instance, to carry on an intellectual profession—may often be recognized as a sublimated modification of this repressed wish.

And Karl Abraham:

> A considerable number of women are unable to carry out a full psychical adaptation to the female role. [Such women may become homosexual or] their homosexuality . . . the repressed wish to be male . . . is to be found in a sublimated form in masculine pursuits of an intellectual and professional character.

Or Helene Deutsch:

> Woman's intellectuality is to a large extent paid for by the loss of valuable feminine qualities: it feeds on the sap of the affective life. . . . the intellectual woman is masculinized; in her, warm, intuitive knowledge has yielded to cold, unproductive thinking. . . . [George Sand] led a very promiscuous life and ruined many men.[19]

What are the possible female responses to these varieties of denial of agency?—*she couldn't have written it* (or painted it, for that matter), *she stole it, she's really a man, only a woman who is more-than-a-woman could have done it,* or *she did write it but look how immodest it makes her, how ridiculous, how unlovable, how abnormal!* Faced with inferiority on the one hand, and on the other, varying degrees of ruin of her personal life, a woman could respond like Gwen Raverat, who (says Elizabeth Janeway) "could not imagine actually being a famous painter; the most she could dream of was marrying one":

> I should have liked . . . to be Mrs. Rembrandt but that seemed too tremendous even to imagine; whereas it did not seem impossibly outrageous to think of myself as Mrs. Bewick. . . . Surely, I thought, if I cooked his roast beef beautifully and mended his clothes and minded the children—surely he would, just sometimes, let me draw and engrave a little tailpiece for him. . . . I wouldn't sign it.[20]

For others there is the position of abject surrender, possibly in hopes of being admitted to the club as token; thus, Marya Mannes in an advertisement as late as 1967: "Charles Jackson has had the guts to create a heroine who loves men more than herself and is honest enough to admit it."[21]

An article Mannes published earlier, in 1963, shows the confusions and compromises a woman can be forced into even when what she is protesting is her own situation. Declaring her intention in "Problems of Creative Women" to "think radically," and protesting "the relentless, steady nudging of society" that pushes all women into "stereotyped femininity," Mannes is not really talking about all women (as she is careful to point out). Rather she subscribes to the same doctrine of "sexual duality" as Otto Weininger, believing that "a woman can be 70 to 60 percent

female to 30 to 40 percent male and still function biologically."
Thus "equality is not at issue. . . . what is at issue is the recognition of minorities." Although protesting against women's
impossible double work-load, her only reply is to invoke an
idealized and false past: "Nobody expected George Eliot to be
a beauty. Nobody worried about Jeanne d'Arc's haircut. Emily
Dickinson was not scorned for being childless." (In fact, George
Eliot's biographer describes her heartbreak at her plainness;
one of the accusations persistently brought against Joan at her
trial was her wearing of male attire; and as for childlessness, see
Moore's poem to Harriet Martineau.) Although Mannes believes
her "minority to be in the vanguard of the revolution," these
women who "can love men yet not submerge themselves in
men; can love children but not dedicate themselves to them;
can enjoy domesticity but not devote themselves to it; can be
feminine but not make a fetish of it" [a fairly tame revolution, it
seems] can only delay marriage, hope for the rare, lucky, sensitive husband, endure loneliness, accept a double burden of work
and guilt and "the lonely few of us will just have to go on."[22]

Mannes' article has its sadness, but for some the response is
conflict or open anger. Tillie Olsen points to a letter Sylvia
Plath wrote as a graduate student: ". . . a woman has to sacrifice
all claims to femininity and family to be a writer." And here is
Olsen's account of Elizabeth Mann Borghese, Thomas Mann's
daughter:

> sent to a psychiatrist for help in getting over an unhappy
> love affair revealing also an . . . ambition to become a great
> musician although "women cannot be great musicians."
> "You must choose between your art and fulfillment as a
> woman," the analyst told her, "between music and family
> life." "Why?" . . . "Why must I choose? No one said to Tos-
> canini or Bach or my father, that they must choose between

their art and fulfillment as a man, family life. . . . Injustice everywhere."[23]

For some, the reaction is intense despair. Here is Miriam Henderson, in the early part of the nineteenth century:

> If one could only burn all the volumes, stop the publication of them. But it was all books, all the literature in the world, right back to Juvenal. . . . Education would always mean coming in contact with that. . . . *How* could Newnham and Girton women endure it? How could they go on living and laughing and talking? . . . There is no pardon possible for man. The only answer to them is suicide; all women ought to agree to commit suicide.[24]

But some survive; "Miriam Henderson" is actually a character of Dorothy Richardson's, and Richardson wrote much and died in 1957 at the age of eighty-four. Gwen Raverat did marry a painter—but she also became one, says Janeway, "by absolute refusal to act the expected role of charming young lady. This condemned her to live the formative years of her youth crosswise to custom and approval, odd-girl-out. . . . One must want something very much to go through that."[25] And Sylvia Plath wrote, at least until her suicide at the age of thirty-one.

So they write. And they paint. And let's (for the moment) discount the idiocies of the various forms of denial of agency and pollution thereof; most critics, male or female, will not declare a work bad ipso facto because its authorship is female, or indulge in the indecencies of pollution of agency by declaring the author per se improper, ridiculous, abnormal, and so on.

.   What then?

5.
The Double Standard
of Content

CRITICS WHO ARE TOO SENSIBLE to succumb to some version of *She didn't write it* and too decent to resort to the (always rather snide) *She did, but she shouldn't have* can often find other ways to dismiss the tuneful yodelling and graceful ice-sliding of those wrongly shaped—or wrongly tinted—Glotolog who somehow persist in producing art despite the obstacles arrayed against them. Motives for the dismissal differ: habit, laziness, reliance on history or criticism that is already corrupt, ignorance (the most excusable of all, surely), the desire not to disturb the comfort based on that ignorance (much less excusable), the dim (or not-so-dim) perception that one's self-esteem or sex-based interests are at stake, the desire to stay within an all-male, all-white club that is, whatever its drawbacks, familiar and comfortable, and sometimes the clear perception that letting outsiders into the club, economically or otherwise, will disturb the structure of quid pro quo that keeps the club going. For example,

Podhoretz makes it clear that Susan Sontag became a critic because of "the . . . availability of *a* vacant position in the culture . . . Dark Lady of American Letters" (italics mine). As Elaine Reuben notes:

> For a woman below the *Grande Dame* it would seem there has been only one female role in the (male) world of culture, and the nature of that role is such that there can be only one Dark Lady per party. Or even per generation.[1]

Mary McCarthy (who had, according to Podhoretz, "carved out" the position of Dark Lady for herself) explains the beginning of her critical career thus:

> . . . the magazine . . . had accepted me unwillingly . . . because I had a minute "name" and *was the girl friend of one of the "boys," who had issued a ukase on my behalf.* . . . The field assigned to me was the theatre, because, just before this, *I had been married to an actor.* . . . Some of the editors felt that *the theater was not worth bothering with.* . . . But this was an argument for letting me do it. If I made mistakes, who cared? . . . nobody had much confidence in my powers as a critic.[2] [italics mine]

McCarthy's account of her professional debut resembles that of one of the editors of *Titters,* recently interviewed on television (by *Woman,* produced in Buffalo, NY); the interviewee was admitted to the staff of the *National Lampoon* because she was "going with" one of the male editors.

If a woman or any other outsider does not fit at all into the (white male) quid pro quo of the group, getting in can be tougher. I am reminded of a small western college in which a friend of mine taught the writing of fiction; she was on leave and about to leave. The (otherwise all-male) writing program, having secured a male substitute for one year, proceeded to argue that his contract must be extended another two; it was not fair to him; he had a family to support; and so on—opposed only by the one woman on the committee, who kept pointing out that an extension of contract would be not only unethical but illegal. The committee, as its clinching piece of evidence, revealed to the woman who opposed the appointment that they had already promised him the job. (He got it.)

Needless to say, the crescent-finned and other Glotolog usually face critics more ethical—but often more confused—than this. The Double Standard of Content is perhaps the fundamental weapon in the armory and in a sense the most innocent, for men and women, whites and people of color do have very different experiences of life and one would expect such differences to be reflected in their art. I wish to emphasize here that I am not talking (vis-à-vis sex) about the relatively small area of biology—about this kind of difference in experience, men are often curious and genuinely interested—but about socially enforced differences. The trick in the double standard of content is to label one set of experiences as more valuable and important than the other. Thus we have added to *She didn't write it* and *She did, but she shouldn't have*, a third piece of denigration: *She did, but look what she wrote about.*

Here is Virginia Woolf, defining the business with her usual clarity (and adding to experience the matter of values, which flows from it):

> . . . the values of women differ very often from the values . . . [of men] naturally this is so. Yet it is the masculine values that prevail. Speaking crudely, football and sport are "important"; the worship of fashion, the buying of clothes "trivial." And these values are inevitably transferred from life to fiction.

This is an important book, the critic assumes, because it deals with war. This is an insignificant book because it deals with the feelings of women in a drawing-room. A scene in a battlefield is more important than a scene in a shop.[3]

Thirty-nine years later Mary Ellmann can speak of

the most familiar and reliable of all comments on women novelists. Their experience is narrow, their characters never leave "the bedroom and the salon" (alternate phrasing, "boudoir and parlor"). It is also customary to speak of these rooms as "hermetically sealed." Women are incapable of dealing with such airy spaces as Wall Street or the Pentagon.[4]

Many feminists argue that the automatic devaluation of women's experience and consequent attitudes, values, and judgments springs from an automatic devaluation of women per se, the belief that manhood is "normative" and womanhood somehow "deviant" or "special." Such a belief, says Phyllis Chesler

allows men to *not* experience female suffering as representative of *human*—and therefore male—suffering. Female suffering is . . . less pertinent, less significant, less threatening than the pain which befalls men.[5] [italics Chesler's]

Can these contentions be proved? I think they can. For example, one of the victims of the double standard of content is Virginia Woolf herself, who writes earlier in A *Room of One's Own*: "all these good novels, *Villette, Emma, Wuthering Heights, Middlemarch*, were written by women without more experience of life than could enter the house of a respectable clergyman."[6]

But she does not go on to say, although it's true, that the sort of heroine George Eliot drew is precisely the sort Tolstoy (whom she later mentions for the breadth of *his* experience) could not even see, let alone delineate, that the schoolgirls of *Villette* are a truth no male novelist had even guessed at, that in short the women confined to the houses of respectable clergymen knew not *less* than their brothers and fathers but *other* and that if the women did not know what the men knew, it is just as true to say that the men did not know what the women knew—and what the men did not know included *what the women were.* Woolf is here the victim of the fallacy she herself describes. Victorian women's experience is "narrow" in terms of the experience of Victorian men, true, but so is Victorian men's in terms of Victorian women's. As late as 1935 Lord David Cecil chides Marian Evans for succumbing to "the frailties of her sex; like every woman novelist, she tends to draw heroes . . . in the image of her desire."[7] Quotations from feminist critics bent on returning the compliment to male authors would fill a book; let me merely quote a contemporary critic, Judith Fetterley, who sums it up: "the amount of nonsense in poetry on the subject of myself is simply overwhelming."[8]

Not only is female experience often considered less broad, less representative, less important, than male experience, but the actual content of works can be distorted according to whether the author is believed to be of one sex or the other. Thus in 1847 a novel appeared in England by a new and unknown writer. Reviewers found it "powerful and original," says Carol Ohmann. Its "essential subject was taken to be a representation of cruelty, brutality, violence . . . wickedness in its most extreme forms. . . . reviewers were variously displeased, inclined to be melancholy, shocked, pained, anguished, disgusted and sickened [but] a number . . . allowed the novel to be the work of a promising, possibly great, new writer." According to Ohmann, Percy Edwin Whipple of the *North American Review* found the novel's hero "bestial, brutal, indeed monstrous." The author was "spendthrift of malice and profanity." In the *American Review* George Washington Peck called the language that of a "Yorkshire farmer or a boatman or of frequenters of 'barrooms and steamboat saloons.'" The author he called "a rough sailor" who did not understand women and did not see them as they were. In 1850 the novel appeared in a second edition, its authorship became known, and although not one comma of the text was thereby changed, the subject matter underwent an immediate and mysterious transformation. For one thing brutal realism becomes "a self-consistent monster" to the reviewer of the *Athenaeum*, who then spends most of his 2,000 words on the author's life, not the novel. In the *Palladium*, Sydney Dobell, who had guessed the authorship three months previously, called the novel a love story and stressed "the youthfulness of the author [whom] he likened . . . to a little bird fluttering its wings against the bars of its cage." The *North American Review* finds the book's "peculiarity or strangeness mirrors the 'distorted' fancy of the writer's life, which was isolated and deprived." Twentieth-century critics continue to see the novel as written involuntarily by a naïve author (Mark Schorer), or as an imperfectly controlled work (Thomas Moser) whose real subject is the hero's "magical sexual power" but which undergoes "femininization" in the second half and a falling-off in artistry. The novelist is again writing involuntarily and did not "consciously" accept the novel's true subject. Ohmann assures us: "I could go on—to essays by Lord David Cecil, Richard Chase, Elliott Gose, Albert Guerard, James Hafley, Harry Levin, C. Day Lewis, Wade Thompson, and even Arnold Kettle, and the list would still not be complete."

The novel? Emily Brontë's *Wuthering Heights*. As Carol Ohmann puts it, "there is a considerable correlation between what readers assume or know the sex of the writer to be and what they actually see or neglect to see in 'his' or her work."[9]

A woman *cannot* write about evil like a coarse Yorkshire boat-man; therefore she *did* not; therefore the novel *must be* a love story and a "self-consistent monster." This view of *Wuthering Heights* must perforce find Heathcliff's sadism and the story of the second generation (Cathy Linton and Hareton Earnshaw) embarrassing; the 1939 film with Merle Oberon and the handsome young Laurence Olivier agreed with Thomas Moser; they lit Olivier beautifully, deleted his cruelty, and drastically compressed the last half of the novel. *TV Guide* for the week of July 24, 1978, went even further, calling the film "Emily Bronte's haunting tale of the tragic romance between a materialistic girl ... and a proud stable-boy. ... A masterpiece" (p. A-60).

It would be nice to think that the exaltation of male authorship via the derogation of female authorship is dying out. In 1975, however, Robert Silverberg, a well-known writer and (to my mind) excellent editor of science fiction, introduced the collected works of a new, unknown, and pseudonymous fellow writer as follows:

> there is to me something ineluctably masculine about Tiptree's writing ... his work is analogous to that of Hemingway ... that prevailing masculinity about both of them— that preoccupation with questions of courage, with absolute values, with the mysteries and passions of life and death as revealed by extreme physical tests.[10]

In 1977 it was revealed that James Tiptree Jr. was the pen name of a sixty-one-year-old retired biologist named Alice Sheldon— who had found a pseudonym she fancied on a jar of marmalade while shopping in the supermarket.

In 1848 Percy Edwin Whipple of the *North American Review* believed *Jane Eyre* to have been written by a brother and sister, the brother contributing everything but the "feminine peculiarities" of "elaborate descriptions of dress," "the minutiae of the sick-chamber," and "various superficial refinements of feeling."[11] In 1974 author Suzy McKee Charnas sent a mailing about her first published novel to a group of feminist bookstores. One of them, she says,

> turned out to be not feminist but mixed-radical.... a man wrote a reply. He protested that SF is not mostly junk because it is a male ghetto, but that each sex has its strengths to contribute—men's strength being plot and women's character.[12]

The double standard of experience in fiction hurts all women artists, both those whose art is specifically, recognizably "feminine" (it is depreciated) and those whose art is not (it is misinterpreted). And in both cases the genuineness of what in fact constitutes the author's experience—and her art—vanishes. Thus Stephen Spender can tell us that Wilfrid Owen's "warning ... came out of the peculiar circumstances of the trenches" [while] "with Sylvia Plath, her femininity is that her hysteria comes completely out of herself."[13] Mary Ellmann comments that Sylvia Plath never received shock treatment; even that came from her own "hysteria."[14]

Perhaps a personal anecdote will serve to make clearer what I mean by the relation of female experience to female art and both to male ignorance. Some years ago I served as the one woman on a committee of three professors of writing; our job was to screen candidates for an MA program in creative writing. As we proceeded in our tedious and unpleasant chore of reading perhaps two hundred manuscripts, some interesting facts emerged:

> —Our rankings of the top 50 percent of the manuscripts were almost identical.

—My ranking of the top twenty samples of the prose and verse written by men was almost identical with my colleagues'.

—My ranking of the top twenty samples of the prose and verse written by women was almost exactly the inverse of theirs.

I remember in particular a short story, funny and classically feminist, which ended with the female protagonist lying in bed next to her sleeping husband, wishing she had the courage to hit him over the head with a frying pan. That last detail is distinctive; I suspect the story appeared later in a feminist literary magazine. My colleagues, who did not like the story, could not understand why the protagonist was so angry; my explanations (which connected the story with feminist consciousness) brought from one only the polite but baffled response that the story was about "a failure in human communications" in that particular marriage.

The other manuscript I remember very well was a poem I found impressive and will try to reconstruct from memory. A fifteen-year-old girl, after a date with a boy she didn't like, "so I had to work at it," returns (alone) to "my mother's kitchen," opens the gleaming, white refrigerator and finds that something startling has happened—the interior of the refrigerator has miraculously (and spontaneously) become entirely covered with red cabbage roses. As I tried to explain to my two colleagues the extraordinary elements compressed into that last image, I realized that I was speaking again to ignorance. What did they know of the elaborate rating-dating scheme fifteen-year-old girls went through, of the wrench that occurs in puberty when one moves out of the female world (mothers and friends) into one with a totally different set of standards, a world one must "work at" even if one doesn't like it, so that coming back to the familiar, women's world ("my mother's kitchen," not "*the* kitchen") can be a great relief? Or of the gleaming, white refrigerator which is only a "sanitary" or "efficient" fake—no laboratory appliance but the fountain of plenty, *my mother* in reality, with its miraculous bloom that is at once emotional, uterine, and the center both of the house and of one's life? The bond between mother and daughter blooms inside technology, in the middle of a world in which relations with men are, alas, not a pleasure but work. The poem is a kind of transubstantiation.

So much for my memories of kitchens, dates, and my mother! But my experience was clearly not theirs. How could it be? And female experience of that sort was sufficiently invisible in literature at that time (it may still be so) to make it impossible that they should recognize it from literary sources. None of the women admitted into the program was my choice. None of my female choices were accepted into the program.

Years later another white, male colleague rejected a short story of mine (sent him at his request for a magazine he was editing) explicitly on the grounds that it did not accurately represent the options open to a female adolescent of the 1950s (a subject he presumably knew more about than I did).

Ignorance is not bad faith. But persistence in ignorance is surely bad faith, from "I'm too tired and don't want to think about it," to "This is interfering with my view of the world so I won't think about it," to "This is interfering with my view of the world, which is the only possible and all-inclusive one, so I needn't think about it." Some male scholars' and writers' puzzlement is honest; some judgment of women's experience is truly vicious, like that of a young professor I met at a cocktail party in 1970 who, upon hearing that I was teaching *Jane Eyre*, said, "What a lousy book! It's just a lot of female erotic fantasies," as if female erotic fantasies were per se the lowest depth to which literature could sink. He was hostile; the harried department chairman whose response was, "I didn't know you were interested in the minor Victorians" was merely thoughtless. Both were acting in bad faith.

Here is a little chronicle of a male journey out of bad faith, or rather, its beginnings. Samuel Delany writes of one of the early days of his marriage in 1961:

> ... suddenly the door burst open and Marilyn [Hacker], dripping wet, came in and plopped down some shopping bundles. "Here." I handed her a pair of my jeans since they were the nearest things to hand.... And in the middle of the growing puddle on the kitchen floor, Marilyn undressed, toweled herself off, and slipped into my pants (we both wore size twenty-eight then!), zipped them up.... slid her hands into the pockets.
>
> "What's the matter?" I asked.
>
> She'd suddenly got the strangest expression. "The pockets...!" she exclaimed. "They're so *big!*"
>
> Then she showed me the pockets in the pair of girls' jeans she'd bought a few weeks ago, and the pockets in her overcoat. And in her skirts. None of them was large enough to accommodate a pack of cigarettes.... The idea that pockets in mens' clothes were functional had never occurred to her. The idea that pockets in women's clothing were basically decorative had never occurred to me. We began to talk ... and before long we realized that, although we had gone to the same high school, had seen each other daily for four years, had shared thousands of intimate conversations ... we had been raised in two totally different cultures.[15]

Women's clothes, by the way, still do not have functional pockets, a fact which may be reflected in women's writing. Ellen Moers says:

women writers have women's bodies, which affect their senses and their imagery. They are raised as girls and thus have a special perception of the cultural imprinting of childhood. They are assigned roles in the family and in courtship, they are given or denied access to education and employment, they are regulated by laws of property and political representation which absolutely in the past, partially in the present, differentiate women from men.... The great writers [employ] ... the deep creative strategies of the literary mind at work upon the fact of being female.[16]

If women's experience is defined as inferior to, less important than, or "narrower" than men's experience, women's writing is automatically denigrated.

If women's experience is simply not seen, the effect will be the same.

She wrote it but look what she wrote about becomes *She wrote it, but it's unintelligible/badly constructed/thin/spasmodic/uninteresting,* etc., a statement by no means identical with *She wrote it, but I can't understand it* (in which case the failure might be with the reader). Behind *She wrote it, but it's unintelligible* lies the premise: *What I don't understand doesn't exist*, like Sylvia Plath's "hysteria" which came "completely out of herself," or the woman trying to get into our MA program who could not possibly want to beat "her" husband over the head with a frying pan unless there was "a failure of communication" in that particular marriage.

The social invisibility of women's experience is not "a failure of human communication." It is a socially arranged bias persisted in long after the information about women's experience is available (sometimes even publicly insisted upon).

It is (although the degree thereof varies from circumstance to circumstance) bad faith.

6.
False Categorizing

T IS BAD FAITH that stands behind what I shall call Denial by False Categorizing, a complicated now-you-see-it-now-you-don't sleight of hand in which works or authors are belittled by assigning them to the "wrong" category, denying them entry into the "right" category, or arranging the categories so the majority of "wrong" Glotolog fall into the "wrong" category without anyone's having to do anything further about the matter. False categorizing ranges from the mythologizing assumptions that prevent clear seeing (what Margaret Mead calls the precedence of the dream), to biased misjudgment, to plain lying; at its worst it is the deliberate renaming of phenomena so as to change their significance. Mead's example: "... American soldiers in Europe in World War II looked with perfect honesty at British slums and said, 'No American lives like that.' ... People in America of course live in all sorts of fashions because they are foreigners, or unlucky, or depraved, or without ambition ... but *Americans* live in white detached houses with green shutters. Rigidly, blindly, the dream takes precedence."[1] For the worst sort of renaming with ill intent, one can go to Petersen and Wilson's *Women Artists*, especially the removal of women artists from that category to the category of mothers, wives, daughters, or lovers of men who are artists. Thus: "Sabina von Steinbach . . . worked in the early fourteenth century on the south portal of Strasbourg Cathedral . . . when Erwin, the master builder, died (it is later generations that cast her as his daughter) the contract was given to Sabina." Thus Suzanne Valadon "is usually mentioned in art history texts as the mother of Utrillo." One of the funniest (and most excusable) examples of false categorizing in art history may well be the society column reporting one of Mary Cassatt's rare visits to the United States: "Mary Cassatt, sister of Mr. Cassatt, president of the Pennsylvania Railroad, returned from Europe yesterday. She has been studying painting in Europe and owns the smallest Pekingese dog in the world." In her 1976 lecture in Boulder, J. J. Wilson also mentioned one critic who called Cassatt Degas' pupil—although the two actually met at a one-woman showing of Cassatt's work. And there is also the (let us hope) apocryphal story of the high school textbook which called Marie Curie the "laboratory assistant of her husband, Pierre." Moreover, according to the editors:

> We discovered that if we looked up the family names of well-known male artists—say, Diego Rivera, Jacopo Robusti, Tintoretto, Jean Honoré Fragonard, Pieter Brueghel, Vincent van Gogh, Alexander Calder, Max Ernst, Marcel Duchamp—we often found some account of a wife/lover/sister/mother/daughter who was an artist, too. [and in a footnote] These names . . . could have been expanded from John Singleton Copley to Yves Tanguy—each of them is connected with a woman artist . . . [e.g.,] van Gogh's mother, Anna Cornelia

Carbentus. *One of the Freudian critics does mention her* . . . she loved nature and wrote very well; she also showed ability at drawing. . . . In fact his [van Gogh's] nephew tells us that van Gogh's very first paintings were actual copies of her works.[2] [italics mine]

It takes a Freudian, hypothesizing about Vincent's "identification with his mother," even to mention that she painted.

And here, with some information about music, is Cynthia Fuchs Epstein:

I recently discovered in a biography of Gustav Mahler . . . that his wife was an important assistant who often did orchestration for him. A composer before their marriage, Alma Mahler was forbidden by her husband to write music. Mendelssohn's sister, also a composer, apparently wrote songs which are credited to her brother.

Thus women may not only be renamed as non-artists; their contributions to art may be absorbed into a man's and recategorized as his (apparently on the Blackstonian theory that the two are one person). Epstein adds:

I have begun to collect gracious acknowledgments to wives which indicate the intellectual contribution of the wife to a piece of work, but which do not give professional credit to her. An early example is the acknowledgment of Gabriel Kolko . . . in *Wealth and Power in America* (Praeger, paperback edition, 1967) which states: "To my wife, Joyce, I owe a debt that mere words cannot express. This book is in every sense a joint enterprise and the first in a series of critical studies on which we're presently engaged" (p. xi). . . . the wife did not appear as co-author or junior author.[3]

(The first paperback edition of Eric Berne's *Games People Play* bears a similar dedication, and those interested in specifically literary versions of the games people play about wealth and power in America—or at least credit for work done—may consult Nancy Milford's biography of Zelda Fitzgerald.)

Often the women's work is totally absorbed, for the simplest kind of recategorizing is from the category of things which exist to that of things which do not. The grossest example of this technique that I can find is (luckily) outside literature; in the late Jacob Bronowski's television series *The Ascent of Man*, not only have Hypatia, Marie Curie, Lise Meitner, Lady Augusta Lovelace, Emmy Noether, et al., vanished into thin air, but the following grotesque scene takes place (described by Suzy Charnas):

> [in] the interview that closed the first segment of . . . The Ascent of Guess Who . . . an anthropologist or archaeologist was asked . . . whether there wasn't SOMETHING that had been invented by prehistoric women. He opined that there sure was: the idea of bringing back home some of the berries and things they gathered instead of gobbling them up on the spot, and sharing the goodies with the folks back home. Presumably the (male) hunters were not capable of originating this tender, nurturant behavior, ate up everything that they killed right there, leaving the women and children to starve, so they all died off and none of us are alive today. . . . [Bronowski's] whole intellectual perception of the world simply seems to have excluded women. How can such a creature even begin to see straight?[4]

Vonda McIntyre remarks:

> [on] the Ascent of You Know Who . . . this incredibly famous anthropologist was displaying a very old bone chip with

rows of scratches on it, to demonstrate that paleolithic "man" had a concept of time and numbers. "You see," says he, "this bone has exactly 31 scratches and is obviously a record of the lunar month."

Do tell. A 31-day lunar month? ... I think [it] a good deal more likely [that] the bone was a record of a woman's menstrual cycle.[5]

Not all false categorizing is as blatant as the doesn't-exist school; here is Harold Clurman, writing about the Yiddish Theatre in 1978. He describes the performers as

a host of powerful stars. . . . There was the *majestic* Jacob Adler, the *matinee idol* Boris Thomashefsky, the *formidably emotional* David Kessler; among the women Sarah Adler, Bertha Kalish, Bessie Thomashefsky *were no less striking.* [italics mine]

Clurman not only describes the women as a group (in relation to the men); he then goes on to describe the types of roles each man played, adds an anecdote about a woman in the audience ripping her clothes off during a performance by Boris Thomashefsky, crying, "He is my king," and ends: "*All* these actors radiated unmistakable sexual vitality . . ." (italics mine).[6]

The above are random samples; to collect a systematic account of such false categorizings in literature would take too much time, too much energy, and bars to protect one (as Woolf put it) "of solid gold"; the subject also tends to spread into every other kind of misinterpretation. Here are only two specific areas in which literary renamings are especially capable of abuse: the use of the word *regionalism* and the idea of *genre.*

For example, why was Kate Chopin (until rediscovered by feminists) considered a *regionalist* and not a *realist* or a *sexual pioneer?* Why was Willa Cather described to me twenty years ago in college as a *regionalist* (whereupon I did not read her) while Sherwood Anderson was not a *regionalist?* More pointedly, if Cather (who concentrates on several large, western states) is a *regionalist,* why is Faulkner (who concentrates on one, small southern county) not a *regionalist?* What on earth *is* a regionalist? If "regionalism" means concentration on one geographical area, is Thomas Wolfe a regionalist for writing so much about New York City?

If seems clear that the label *regionalist,* so often applied to women writers, indicates not only that the writer in question concentrates on a particular region, but also that the work is thereby limited (and not of "broad" interest) and therefore of interest not primarily for literary reasons but for its sociological or quasi-historical interest. The "regionalist" is a second-rate fictioneer, a documentary-maker manqué(e).

The assignment of *genre* can also function as false categorizing, especially when work appears to fall between established genres and can thereby be assigned to either (and then called an imperfect example of it) or chided for belonging to neither. In 1971 three white women (one of whom told me this story) were putting together a course in the contemporary novel for a small, western college. Hesitating between James Baldwin and George Orwell, they finally rejected the former and included the latter, despite the fact that Baldwin was a fellow-countryman of their students and could presumably speak more directly to them than the British Orwell.

But Baldwin (they said) was *not a novelist.* This judgment is especially striking in that the mixture of fiction and nonfiction in the works of both is almost identical. But one cannot teach Baldwin's work without dealing with American racism and homophobia, while Orwell's dislike of British imperialism is safely distant and much of his work can be taught (inaccurately) as anti-Communist. How much easier it was, rather than confronting one's own fear and discomfort, to make the apparently "neutral" judgment that *Orwell is a novelist; Baldwin is not a novelist.*

Ellen Moers claims that Mary Wollstonecraft is "one of the great prose writers of the language. . . . had she lived beyond the age of thirty-eight, she would have made a major contribution, *perhaps in the novel*" (italics added). She adds that *The Wrongs of Woman; or, Maria* contains Wollstonecraft's "most powerful writing on a woman's passion." Yet when Moers wants to demonstrate that Wollstonecraft is a fine prose writer, she quotes not from the novels but from Wollstonecraft's private letters.[7]

Don't letters count? Real letters, written to real people? Many feminists have begun to argue that much of women's writing exists in the form of letters and diaries—not self-conscious, ritually "literary" ones like Anaïs Nin's (which are accepted, I suspect, for just those qualities) but really private ones, like Pepys'. Do diaries count?

And here is the single most virulent false categorizing ever invented: the moving of art object X from the category of "serious art" to the category of "not serious." A recent television biography of Scott Joplin emphasized his bitterness at never being accepted as a "serious" or publicly honored composer—in contrast with the equally popular (but white) John Philip Sousa. The (also white) George Gershwin was honored during his own short lifetime for bridging the gap between "jazz" and "classical" music; it took Joplin more than fifty years after his death (which was decades after Gershwin's) to gain public recognition. One cannot escape the impression that in Joplin's case the category "not serious" hid another category (which only one character in the television play speaks aloud): "coon music."[8]

A colleague of mine once attempted to have her university buy a lesbian novel by the contemporary lesbian writer Jane

Rule. The response: "We don't want too many *Canadian* novelists" (italics mine). (Which category is being insulted here is something of a puzzle.)

The editors of *Poets of the English Language* (my college textbook for a survey of English poetry), W. H. Auden and Norman Holmes Pearson, tell us that

> critical opinion as to which are the greatest masterpieces or upon the division between major and minor work remains substantially the same at all times . . . on the other hand . . . the relative positions of writers of the second rank are always varying *slightly*.[9] [italics mine]

Alas, neither Aphra Behn nor Margaret Cavendish is even minor; they are nonexistent in *Poets of the English Language*. Aphra Behn may be missing because of male bias (Auden and Pearson may not have approved of women who wrote poems about premature ejaculation) but even Virginia Woolf shakes her head at Cavendish:

> What a vision of loneliness and riot . . . as if some giant cucumber had spread itself over all the roses and carnations in the garden and choked them to death . . . [she] frittered her time away scribbling nonsense and plunging ever deeper into obscurity and folly.[10]

Yet perhaps the Duchess's only folly in modern eyes is writing between genres (as did many of her contemporaries, by the way; the dialogue or romance was then still a common form for what she was writing—which is, by and large, natural philosophy). I have Dolores Palomo's word for it that John Baptista Van Helmont, the father of modern chemistry, had an infinitely worse prose style.[11] Cavendish might, of course, be a bad or indifferent scientist, but that is for a historian of science to decide, not a literary critic. Behind Woolf's judgment of her is an assumption about what she ought to be writing, that is, a misuse of the idea of genre. And what about those odd literary ghettoes in which women so often write: children's books, "Gothics," science fiction, detective stories? Did even feminists consider Dorothy Sayers a "serious" twentieth-century novelist until they discovered *Gaudy Night?* I know many who didn't (I was one).

The younger students are, the worse the kinds of false categorizing they are likely to meet. *Poets of the English Language* (which I was given as a college text) omitted Elizabeth Barrett Browning and Aphra Behn from its pages (while including, for example, Hartley Coleridge) but at least it let its female poets—Anne Bradstreet, the Countess of Winchilsea, Emily Brontë, Christina Rossetti, and Emily Dickinson (five out of one hundred)—remain in the category "poet." In high school I was given—as a prize for "excellence in English," mind you—Louis Untermeyer's popular anthology *A Treasury of Great Poems*,[12] which included six women (if you don't count the ten women out of fifty-eight poets included in the twentieth-century section, a period *Poets of the English Language* did not cover). The book is a mine of false categorizing. Thus: Aphra Behn the poet becomes Aphra Behn the Whore, a sort of Mata Hari ("The enemy succumbed to her. She had no difficulty in extracting secret information"), coarse, "exotic," and a "center of scandal" (p. 514).

Anne Finch, Countess of Winchilsea, the poet, is transformed into the Delicate Bit of Porcelain: "If . . . [she] cannot shake the reader with passion, she can charm him . . . with small felicities." After omitting all of her feminist lines—and her melancholy ones, too—Untermeyer goes on to assure us "her lines . . . owe nothing . . . to a fever in the blood" (pp. 521–522).

Elizabeth Barrett Browning the poet becomes Elizabeth the Wife. "When Robert Browning stormed into her life . . ." and so on until "[Browning's love] was rewarded by countless tributes, preeminently by *Sonnets from the Portuguese*" [the only poems of hers he prints]. "The title was an intimate acknowledgment of her husband's playful way of calling her 'my little Portuguese'" (p. 799).

About Emily Brontë the poet, interestingly enough, Untermeyer says almost nothing; perhaps that grim personality unhinged even him. Thus he begins, "It is hard to separate the Brontës," goes on to state (incorrectly) that "Charlotte died as a consequence of childbirth in her fortieth year" (according to one of her biographers she was in the early months of pregnancy when she died, at thirty-eight),[13] that the Brontës assumed names that were "positively masculine" (Charlotte states in her introduction to the second edition of *Wuthering Heights* that the names were *not* positively masculine!), and that "the Brontës created Gondal" (Gondal was Anne and Emily's creation; Charlotte and Branwell created Angria). He allows Emily more "creative intensity" than other women in literature, goes on to call *Wuthering Heights* "the greatest novel ever achieved *by a woman*" (italics mine) and adds (that "self-consistent monster" again!) "Emily Brontë created a dream world, and made it more real than reality" (p. 880).

Christina Rossetti the poet becomes Christina the Spinster; unhappy, she "refused to marry ... [and] became a recluse." And although she is "*one of the few women* whose lyrics and sonnets will survive" (italics mine) her work is nonetheless "limited in range ... slight in form ... it defies analysis" (pp. 939–940).

Emily Dickinson the poet becomes Emily Dickinson the whimsical "Madcap"—a feat Untermeyer manages by omitting such lyrics as "After great pain," "I felt a funeral in my brain," "Frigid and sweet her parting face," and so on. (This may not be his fault; Untermeyer's anthology was compiled before all of Dickinson's work was publicly available.) Although she, like

Christina, was also "abnormally reticent," a recluse, she fell in love with the Reverend Charles Wadsworth, and to him she wrote love poems "among the finest . . . ever written *by a woman*" (pp. 944ff, italics mine).

For six poets Untermeyer has substituted other categories, the familiar, sexist stereotypes of women: Aphra the Whore, Anne the Lady, Elizabeth the Wife, Christina the Spinster, and Emily Dickinson the Madcap (although Emily is really sad and a spinster, too, if you look carefully). Only Emily Brontë eludes recategorizing; her work is, however, qualified by its being "a dream world" and "by a woman" (twice). She is even deprived of individual outline by being "hard to separate" from her siblings, whose lives and deaths take up much of the material supposedly devoted to her. Thus it becomes futile to ask about the category "poet"—how did these writers write?—and instead we learn that whores are promiscuous, ladies delicate, wives devoted (did Untermeyer think "A Curse for a Nation" was written as a love poem to Robert Browning?), spinsters sad, and madcaps whimsical. (The false categorizing of male writers into something other than writers does occur—e.g., Dylan Thomas as Self-Destructive Visionary, Norman Mailer as Tough Jock, Robert Frost as Sage. But these personae are flattering to the ego and freeing as to conduct; what male writer has been transformed by critics into the Sad, Reclusive, Timid Bachelor [solely by reason of not being married] or the Devoted and Submissive Husband [seen as an exemplary figure]? T. S. Eliot did not become the Bank Clerk *instead of* the Poet. The male personae, if they exist, add to the male writer's authority *as poet*; the female personae substituted for the category Writer are in themselves either still indecent [the Whore] or constricting [the Wife, the Spinster, the Lady]. It is also noteworthy that the male personae are directed toward activity in the outside world, while the female [with the titillating but still-punishable exception of the

Whore] are not. The Sexually Liberated Woman [Erica Jong, etc.] strikes me as a modern version of the Whore and just as much a creature of male fantasy. The Crazy Lady [Anne Sexton] is a modern version of the Unhappy Spinster, and hardly an improvement. I refer, of course, to the personae substituted for the writers in question, not the writers themselves.)

Mind you, Untermeyer's intolerableness is not limited to women; if you look up the preface to "Four Negro Spirituals," you will find

> a blend of savagely rhythmic chants and placid Christian hymns.... They are of varying literary merit. But the best of them express ... a deep emotional sincerity [and] a robust, poetic quality ... childlike responses. [p. 1018]

So much for "some of the greatest poets since Homer"! (Needless to say, Untermeyer omits any knowledge that many of the songs had a meaning unsuspected by the slave-owners.) If we follow Untermeyer into the twentieth century we find that Charlotte Mew and Sara Teasdale are nervous and unhappy spinsters (pp. 1060–1061, 1120–1121), Amy Lowell an eccentric and "furious" controversialist for Imagism which is now "a tempest . . . in a shopworn teapot." He adds that her poems are "prim," printing only "Patterns" (pp. 1078–1081). Anna Wickham, a feminist whose bitter feminism Untermeyer actually quotes ("having to keep silent if she would be loved, and for the other privileges of womanhood"), he calls (possibly because she writes about sex) "a lesser D. H. Lawrence" (p. 1117). H. D. "wrote almost entirely of the classical world" (p. 1136), and Hart Crane's "sexual irregularities" are mentioned (without being defined) (p. 1199), while W. H. Auden is "a sensitive lover" (p. 1220). Leonie Adams, Edna Millay, Marya Zaturenska, Elinor Wylie, and Edith Sitwell are discussed as poets (pp. 1203, 1167, 1207–1208, 1131, 1142–1145).

It would be good to think that Untermeyerism—the recategorizing of women writers into sexist stereotypes, feminists
into anti-feminists, lesbian poets into primness, philosophers
(like H. D.) into I don't know what, black slaves into intuitive
children—had stopped. Few critics, certainly, are as obvious
about it as Untermeyer. But here are excerpts from a correspon-
dence of mine with a contemporary writer, Marilyn Hacker,
poet and winner of the National Book Award. In 1977, thirty-five
years after the publication of Untermeyer's anthology, Hacker
wrote:

> We're plotting to put out an H. D. newsletter. . . . [Poet Marie
> Ponsot] showed me a December 1920 number of *Poetry* with
> three beautiful lyrics by Bryher: obviously erotic, obviously
> to a woman, recognizably to H. D. It was very exciting to see
> them . . . *our* past . . . one of the peculiarly vague . . . serial love
> poems in *Red Roses for Bronze* suddenly coalesced when I rec-
> ognized one of its selections as the poem that appears with
> the dedication to the novel *Palimpsest* "to Bryher." [18 June
> 1977]
>
> No critic ever talks about [Bryher] which would be fine
> if all they *did* talk about was the texts of the poems. But
> H. D.'s friendship with Pound, her brief (3 years) marriage to
> Aldington, her short . . . affair-by-correspondence with D. H.
> Lawrence, are *always* talked about. . . . Her relationship (of
> forty years) with Bryher is ignored, often not even referred
> to as an important friendship. One critic mentioned "bisex-
> ual miseries." . . . Almost none of H. D.'s poems and fiction
> about woman-woman relationships or even about women
> heroes are in print. [28 September 1976]

So much for H. D.'s writing only about the classical world! And
"prim" Amy Lowell, it seems, wrote "open Lesbian erotic poems":

Amy Lowell . . . is so often critically described as poor Amy, prevented by fat from having a Fulfilling Life. . . . In fact, Amy Lowell liked actresses. . . . The woman she lived with for the last 15 years of her life (36 to 51) was one, too. Lowell left all her money and her mansion to her. She also wrote dozens of frankly erotic poems to and about her. . . . The lines about barrenness and lying alone in bed at night, which the poor-Amy critics are so fond of quoting, occur in the context of poems about specific quarrels with, or temporary separations from, her lover. [15 September 1976]

If lesbianism in women writers is not allowed to disturb the transformation of the writer into spinster, eccentric, or dreaming *passéiste* (which is Untermeyer's description of H. D.), neither is public activity allowed to disturb the recategorizing of poet into devoted wife:

Millay introduces the persona of the politically conscious and feminism-conscious woman to American poetry. (It is ironic that this persona was also the usual voice of Elizabeth Barrett, who has been re-written into Sleeping Beauty. . . .)

Hacker adds in the same letter:

There are volumes about Plath. . . . There are several books about Marianne Moore (though by no means as many). There are no books or collections of essays about Muriel Rukeyser. The woman poet must be either a . . . sexless, reclusive eccentric, with nothing to say specifically about women, or a brilliant, tragic, tortured suicide. [2 November 1976]

If the recategorizing of poet into exemplary suicide is too far-fetched, there is always the recategorization from existence to

nonexistence, or (if that fails) the relatively new recategorization from "literature" (broad, general, humanistic, universal)
to "women's studies" (narrow, special, political, biased). Here is
Hacker again:

> This week ... an article by Harold Bloom in *The New Republic*,
> a ... capsule review of Poetry Books Published in 1976. He
> didn't mention *one* book by a woman—and he mentioned
> over 20 books, including Best Small Press Book, Best First
> Book, etc. ... in a year that had new books from New York
> trade houses by Audre Lorde, Robin Morgan, Marge Piercy,
> Susan Griffin, Muriel Rukeyser. ... And how many new titles
> from Alice James, Out and Out, Shameless Hussy, etc.? And
> not a *word* about *any* of that, not even to say he didn't like it!
> And in a cassette catalogue I received (in my professional
> capacity [as a teacher]) of recorded lectures, etc.: in the exten-
> sive section on English and American literature, there were,
> in the poetry section, out of 60 titles, lectures on Dickinson,
> Moore, Louise Bogan, and Plath, all given by men. In the novel,
> *nothing!* There were suggested course-unit groups ... about
> 10 of them. The only one that indicated humanity was two-
> sexed was called "Women in Love" (!) ... about a dozen
> works ... every one by a man. But then, *in a completely differ-*
> *ent section of the catalogue* [italics mine] there was "Women's
> Studies" and *there* were cassettes about Colette ... Virginia
> Woolf, and a half-dozen others. [17 November 1976]

The techniques so far discussed are all means of dealing
with one simple idea: *She wrote it.* (That is, the "wrong" person—
in this case, female—has created the "right" value—i.e., art.)
   Denial of Agency: *She didn't write it.*
   Pollution of Agency: *She shouldn't have written it.*
   Double Standard of Content: *Yes, but look what she wrote about.*

False Categorizing: *She is not really she* [an artist] *and it is not really it* [serious, of the right genre, aesthetically sound, important, etc.] *so how could "she" have written "it"?* Or simply: Neither "she" nor "it" exists. (Simple exclusion.) But sometimes it is admitted: *She wrote it.* That is, some "wrong" authors do make it into the canon of the Great, the Permanent, or (at least) the Serious. Does any way remain of distorting or belittling their achievements short of the recategorizing I've discussed?

7.
Isolation

W HEN A WORK or an author (of the "wrong" sort) does make it into the literary canon of the Great, the Permanent, or (at least) the Serious, there remain two ways of distorting the author's achievement. By careful selection it is possible to create what I would like to call *the myth of the isolated achievement*, that is, the impression that although X appears in this history of literature or that curriculum or that anthology, it is only because of one book or a handful of (usually the same) poems, and therefore X's other work is taken to be nonexistent or inferior.

Methods in painting are more gross and hence more easily observable. Petersen and Wilson state, "Exhaustive books on certain periods . . . do include women, though rarely do even expensive books devote their color plates to women's works." Elsewhere they quote Judith Chase, curator of Charleston's Old Slave Mart, who states flatly, "No Afro-American artists have been included in *any* standard art history." However, if one looks away from the "standard art history" to specialized publications, we find that what we have here is not nonexistence, but only the usual false categorizing; *Women Artists* lists six books, the first two recommended by Chase herself, as useful in this area. They are James A. Porter's *Modern Negro Art* (New York: Arno Press, 1969); Cedric Dover's *American Negro Art* (Greenwich, CT: The New York Graphic Society, 1960); Elton C. Fox's *Seventeen Black Artists on Art* (Los Angeles: Contemporary Crafts Publishers, 1969); Elsa Honig Fine, *The Afro-American Artists: A Search for Identity* (New York: Holt, Rinehart, and Winston, 1973); *Afro-American Artists: A Bio-Bibliographical Directory*, compiled and edited by Theresa Dickason Cederholm (Boston: Trustees of the Boston Public Library, 1973); and Ora Williams' *American Black Women in the Arts and Social Sciences: A Bibliographic Survey* (Metuchen, NJ: Scarecrow Press, 1973).[1]

Some literary examples: in the fall of 1974 there were three or four different paperback editions of Mary Shelley's *Frankenstein* in print and on sale in the bookstore of the university where I worked. There was no edition of Shelley's *The Last Man* there or in any other bookstore in town. There was, as it turned out, one edition of *The Last Man* in print in the United States, a relatively expensive edition issued by a university press.[2]

In about 1971 I was teaching Charlotte Brontë in a women's studies course and decided to use her *Villette* instead of *Jane Eyre*. The number of different publishers who have in print different paperback editions of *Jane Eyre* I know not; I found several editions in the bookstore of my university (and one more, a year later, in the "Gothic" section of the local supermarket). But there was not one edition of *Villette* in print in the United States, whether in paperback or hardcover, and I finally had to order the book (in hardcover, too expensive for class use) from England. (The only university library editions of *Villette* or *Shirley* I could find at that time were the old Tauchnitz editions: tiny type and no leading.)

In three women's studies classes in two separate institutions (1972–1974) I have asked my students whether they had read *Jane Eyre*. About half had, in all three classes. Of these only one young woman (almost all of the students were women) knew that Charlotte Brontë had written any other novel, though a considerable number (looking, they explained, for another "Brontë book," had happened upon *Wuthering Heights*). Most of my students who had read *Jane Eyre* had done so in their early teens and most were vague about exactly how they had come to read it, although most were also very clear that it was not through assigned reading in school. It seems to me that these youngsters, who had somehow "found" *Jane Eyre* as part of an amorphous culture outside formal education (librarians? friends?) would have gone on to read *Shirley* and *Villette*—if the books had been physically available to them. But they were not, and Charlotte Brontë remained to them the author of one book, *Jane Eyre*. None of them, of course, knew of Emily Brontë's poems, let alone her Gondal poems.

Another anecdote: a female graduate student in English, to whom I had loaned Ellen Moers' *Literary Women*, burst in, eyes wide, passionately declaring, "You mean she wrote *that?*" "She" turned out to be Elizabeth Barrett Browning and "that" was "A Curse for a Nation," especially the lines,

> A curse from the depths of womanhood
> Is very salt, and bitter, and good.[3]

All she had previously read of EBB's was a few of the *Sonnets from the Portuguese*. She—as I—had been convinced that this author's only good work was a few over-anthologized love poems, that the substitution of Devoted Wife for Poet was true, and that "Aurora Leigh" was a dull, silly piece of journalism manqué whose feminism (if it had any) was timid and dated. (Alas, Woolf herself, taking this view in *The Second Common Reader*, makes subtle fun of a poem she nonetheless confesses apologetically to liking. It is Ellmann's phallic criticism, from the "unnaturally close" connection "between a woman's art and a woman's life" to the emphasis on the constriction of her life necessarily leading to faults in the work.)[4]

I must add, embarrassingly, that I shared my student's reaction, that I assumed *Jane Eyre* to be Brontë's best book (and the others vaguely dull) until a description Kate Millett gave of *Villette* (in *Sexual Politics*)[5] sent me on a hunt for *Villette* which eventually broadened to include *Shirley, The Professor*, Charlotte Brontë's juvenilia, Jane Austen's juvenilia (astonishing Kafkaesque stuff), Fanny Ratchford's books on the Brontës, and Emily Brontë's Gondal poems.

Another confession: three times in my life I have had an aesthetic reaction so intense that my first response was, "Who *is* that?"—at my first hearing of Joplin's "Maple Leaf Rag," at hearing a Carmen who was not only singing but also (impossibly) speaking (it was the early Maria Callas), and at the following lines:

> All my walls are lost in mirrors,
> whereupon I trace
> Self to right hand, self to left hand,
> self in every place,
> Self-same solitary figure, self-same
> seeking face.

These chilling, trancelike, almost schizophrenic lines with their technical brilliancy ("s" is the hardest repeated sound to handle in English; these six lines have thirteen s's—and two z's, for good measure!) could not possibly have been written by the docile spinster whose heart was like a singing bird and who spent her life writing love poems or simple-minded nursery fairytales. Of course they were not; that *persona* (another recate-gorizing) has nothing to do with the real author of the poems, who is the *poet* Christina Rossetti. (Moers connects the above lines to the kind of consciousness shown in Diane Arbus' photo-graphs or Carson McCullers' perceptions of freakishness.)[6]

One might argue—and justly—that many male writers are also represented by only one book or one group of poems. I would answer first that the damage done the women is greater because women constitute so few of the total in anthologies, classes, cur-ricula, and reading lists at any level of education. Moreover, the real mischief of the myth of the isolated achievement, as it is applied to the "wrong" writers, is that the criteria of selection are *in themselves loaded* and so often lead to the choice of whatever in the writer's work will reinforce the stereotypical notion of what women can write or should write. Some unpleasant possibilities:

If a woman writer presents herself as a public, political voice, delete this aspect of her work and emphasize her love poems, declared (on no evidence) to be written to her husband—Elizabeth Barrett Browning.

If a woman writer is frank about heterosexuality, delete any of her work that depicts male inadequacy or independent female judgment of men—Aphra Behn.

If a woman writes homosexual love poetry, suppress it and declare her an unhappy spinster—Amy Lowell.

If you still have trouble, invent an (unhappy) heterosexual affair for her to explain the poems—Emily Dickinson.

If a writer is openly feminist, delete everything of that sort in her work and then declare her passionless, minor, and ladylike—Anne Finch, Countess of Winchilsea.

If she is not easy to edit, writes ten-act plays about women going to war to rescue their men, plays about women's acade-mies becoming more popular than men's academies, and endless prefaces about men, women, sexist oppression, and the mistreatment she herself endures, forget it; she's cracked—Margaret Cavendish, Duchess of Newcastle.

If she writes about women's relationships with women and "women heroes" (in Hacker's phrase), print a few of her early lyrics and forget the rest—H. D.

If she writes about women's experiences, especially the unpleasant ones, declare her hysterical or "confessional"—Sylvia Plath, Anne Sexton.

If she carefully avoids writing about female experience and remains resolutely detached, polished, impersonal, and nonsexual, you may praise her at first, then declare her Mandarin, minor, and passionless—Marianne Moore.

I think it no accident that the myth of the isolated achievement so often promotes women writers' less good work as their best work. For example, *Jane Eyre* exists, as of this writing, on the graduate reading list of the Department of English at the University of Washington. (This is the only PhD reading list to which I have access at the moment. I mention it not as a horrid example, but because it is respectable, substantial, and probably typical of first-rate institutions across this country.) *Villette* does not appear on the list. How could it? *Jane Eyre* is a love story and women ought to write love stories; *Villette*, "a book too subversive to be popular," is described by Kate Millett as "one long meditation on a prison break."[7] And let me remind you of Marilyn Hacker's complaints about the treatment accorded women poets, including simple invisibility in such a prestigious journal as the *New Republic*.

Nor are the more prestigious anthologies exempt. Claudia Van Gerven, examining *The New Oxford Book of American Verse*, compares the choices of the new editor, Richard Ellmann, with those of F. O. Mattiessen, editor of the original *Oxford Book of American Verse*. Thus:

. . . only the most gifted women and minority poets survive. Of an entire generation of women poets, the peers of Pound, Williams, and Eliot, only Marianne Moore and H. D. remain. . . . Amy Lowell, Elinor Wylie, and Edna St. Vincent Millay [originally represented], all are omitted. Ellmann . . . adds several women . . . but all [except for Phyllis Wheatley, Elizabeth Bishop, and Jean Garrigue] . . . were too young to be included in Mattiessen's 1950 edition.

Van Gerven goes on to note that since, in both editions:

only contemporary women poets are represented in any number it becomes clear that a woman must be extraordinary to outlive her generation—And that a man need not. . . . several relatively minor figures of [Lowell, Wylie, and Millay's] . . . generation are retained . . . Vachel Lindsay, John Crowe Ransom, Allen Tate, and Ivor Winters.

One might, of course, quarrel with the above judgment of Ellmann's choices. But the way in which Ellmann minimizes the achievements of the women he does include is another matter; nor is Mattiessen innocent of the same kind of recategorizing. Thus:

He [Ellmann] dispatches . . . Anne Bradstreet and Phyllis Wheatley easily since he treats them as "firsts." . . . The first American to publish and . . . the first female slave.

Similarly, Mattiessen includes H. D. and Amy Lowell

only because of their involvement with the imagist school— a school whose limitations are evident in the poetry of these women, Mattiessen contends.

Emily Dickinson, one might think, is hard to use either as a "first" or as illustrating the limitations of a school. Indeed, Ellmann praises Dickinson highly; she "offered the second great innovative reinterpretation of life during the nineteenth century in America" (along with Whitman, who offered the first). But there is nonetheless something wrong with Emily and something right with Walt; she had no influence on anyone while he did:

> [Ellmann] claims that Dickinson had "no influence during her life" because "her poems were unpublished," and that she had "little influence later, because imitating her was not easy." While Ellmann . . . assumes that Whitman could influence "even poets who did not read him" and that he could "electrify" Yeats and Hopkins even though he was not "emulated directly."

This is double-think with a vengeance. The irony increases when we find out that Amy Lowell—whom Mattiessen included in the original collection but Ellmann dropped—has written a poem, "Sisters," in which she directly acknowledges her debt to Dickinson, and Adrienne Rich does likewise in a poem ("I Am in Danger—Sir") *which Ellmann has included in his own, revised collection.*[8] I find it hard to escape the conclusion that "influence" here means influence on men but not on women, possibly because women are not really poets and don't count—a recategorizing we have seen before.

What happens at the Oxford University Press is reflected at lower levels. As we have seen, *She wrote it, but she only wrote one of it* or *She wrote it, but there are practically none of her,* also leads to *She wrote it, but it has only one, limited kind of importance*—this is what Van Gerven is saying when she discusses Ellmann's treating Phyllis Wheatley and Anne Bradstreet as "firsts" or Mattiessen's inclusions of H. D. and Amy Lowell as illustrations of the specific technical characteristics (and defects) of a particular school. In a study of women writers in freshman English anthologies—i.e., textbooks used to teach composition, not literature—Jean S. Mullen has found the following statistics: first, that the proportion of women writers is, oddly enough, about the same as that represented in the University of Washington graduate reading list, *Poets of the English Language*, and *A Treasury of Great Poems*: "about 7% of the total, of which five [texts] were above the average and twelve below it." If we assume that no women wrote before the late seventeenth century and so don't count anyone up to that period, the number of female poets in *Poets of the English Language* is 5 out of 100 (the anthology stops at Yeats, however); *A Treasury of Great Poems* is a heartening 12 out of 98; and the University of Washington's graduate reading list is 8 out of 108, plus 1 woman novelist out of an optional group of 7, and 2 women poets out of an optional group of 8. Second:

> Where *overall examples* of stylistic excellence were offered, male writers predominated to the extent of 98%—women's writing was more likely to be used for specific examples of diction, metaphor, allusion, order and emphasis (up to 12%). Men were presented as *the writers to emulate* while women writers could illustrate useful techniques.

And:

> The same type of discrepancy appeared in linguistic matters. For examples . . . women writers were cited 12 to 17% of the time. But when it came to linguistic principles . . . there were 29 essays by men [and no women].

Unsurprisingly, 6 percent or fewer of the works on self-understanding were by women (the figure soared to 20 percent on marriage), and no works on higher education were by women. Except for sociology and anthropology (25 percent), women had "almost no voice" on philosophical issues about society, little on moral matters (4 percent), none on government, and of seventytwo essays on philosophy, three were by women.[9]

When women writers are falsely categorized as something other than writers, much of their work must be ignored or misinterpreted to make the recategorizing stick. What is left is apt to be dull, since it is not, in fact, part of the writer's central concern. If the writer has the good fortune to fit fairly easily into *what women can write* or *what women should write*, this very fact can be used as an automatic criticism of the work in question.

Faced with such a Catch-22, it is hardly surprising how few women manage to be seen as "great writers." I believe that even those included in the canon suffer from false categorizing, the effect of which is to diminish their work, isolate part of their achievement at the expense of the rest, and expose them to criticism of manufactured, not real, inadequacies. Usually one must infer such a process from one or two pieces of evidence (like the nonexistence of any in-print edition of *Villette* in the United States a few years ago), but in the case of one writer a more detailed look at the process has just come to light, illuminating the degrees of bad faith which combine to make otherwise sane and fairly honest (one supposes) men and women deny the plain evidence of their eyes and ears. Here are some of this mysterious writer's own words:

> Our ideology is still so inveterately anthropocentric that it
> has been necessary to coin this clumsy term . . . to describe

the class whose fathers have been educated at public schools and universities. Obviously if the term "bourgeois" fits ... it is grossly incorrect to use it of one who differs so profoundly in the two prime characteristics of the bourgeoisie—capital and environment.

Or:

[One] ... class possesses in its own right and not through marriage practically all the capital, all the land, all the valuables, and all the patronage in England. [The other] ... class possesses in its own right and not through marriage practically none of the capital, none of the land, none of the valuables, and none of the patronage in England.

Or:

Not only are [they] ... incomparably weaker than the men of our own class ... [they] are weaker than the women of the working class. If the working women of the country were to say: "If you go to war, we will refuse to make munitions or help in the production of goods," the difficulty of war-making would be seriously increased. But if ... [they] were to down tools tomorrow nothing essential ... would be embarrassed. [Their] class is the weakest of all the classes in the state.[10]

Is this Friedrich Engels, perhaps? Or George Bernard Shaw in an uncharacteristically grim mood? Whoever wrote the book the above is taken from is certainly an astonishingly advanced political thinker; if you read further you will find sex treated as a caste, (the ideal of) shared parenting by fathers and mothers, wages proposed for the job of wife and mother, the effortless identification of sexism, capitalism, and war as "the same," and the socialization, psychology, and unpaid labor which lie behind all of them. Whoever this is, it is certainly not Engels or Shaw. Perhaps it is a recent essay of Shulamith Firestone's? Or a new book by Ti-Grace Atkinson? But it's too elegantly written, and it was published in 1938.

Moreover, she (yes, it was a woman) published in the *Daily Worker*. She refused the order of Dame of the British Empire "with a simple and defiant 'No'" ("From Italy, where she was observing Mussolini's fascism first-hand").[11] With war impending, she wrote "as a woman I have no country."[12] She believed in a natural alliance between women and workers.[13] She urged historians to write of the working class. She denounced the killing of the possibility for poetry in the poor.[14] She taught history to working women at Morley College "over the objections of administrators who thought the women should learn more 'practical' subjects like English composition" and "frequently reviewed works on biography, history, and politics." She refused honorary degrees from the University of Manchester and the University of Liverpool out of principle, declined to give the Clarke lectures at Cambridge, and refused to accept the order of the Companion of Honor. She wrote in her diary, "Nothing would induce me to connive at all that humbug." In 1935 the London Library refused to accept women on the Library Committee and a friend baited her about it; she called the very possibility of being invited to serve on the committee that "pail of offal." She worked actively with Margaret Llewellyn Davies' Women's Cooperative Guild, hosted their meetings at her home, and was invited to write the introduction to a collection of memoirs of the lives of working women, published by her own small press in 1931.[15]

The same woman was described by the critic David Daiches near the end of her lifetime, in 1939:

One wonders if Mrs. Woolf's conception of the novel in terms of poetry is not an excuse for remaining in her study. The lyrical mood has many disguises, but at its basis . . . is egotism.

And Quentin Bell, her biographer, writes that her

answer to all this violence lay in an improvement of one's own moral state.

R. L. Chambers holds that:

She is not really interested in what people do. . . . To her the really interesting occurrences are the occurrences of the mind. . . . her attitude towards business [is] as either an esoteric mystery or an opportunity for slumming in an organized way, and by her use of India as a sort of drop-scene . . . very sketchy, which she can call into play whenever she wants to send off a man to *do* something. . . . *she did not know enough* about business and about India. . . . [italics mine]

To this Berenice Carroll, from whose essay on Woolf's political thought I am quoting, answers that Woolf's mother's family included two "high Anglo-Indian administrators," one a member of the Council of the East India Company, and that Leonard Woolf, before his marriage to Virginia, had been District Officer of Hambantota Province in Ceylon. After their marriage he "wrote extensively on British and European imperialism." Certainly Woolf had access to information about British imperialism and India, if she had wanted to use it. But it is apparently incredible to Chambers that she did not want to, although, as Carroll points out, Woolf admonishes women in *Three Guineas* "to maintain an attitude of indifference to men's 'mulberry tree' of war, property and 'intellectual harlotry.'" Worse still,

Chambers observes that Woolf knows little of those "below" her (like the members of the Working Women's Guild?) or treats them with "pure hatred."[16] Chambers' example is Doris Kilman in *Mrs. Dalloway*, but here (it is Carroll's example) is the same kind of woman in *A Room of One's Own*:

> ... to be always doing work that one did not wish to do, and to do it like a slave, flattering and fawning, not always necessarily perhaps, but it seemed necessary and the stakes were too great to run risks.[17]

Even Herbert Marder, as late as 1968 in *Feminism and Art*, concluded that Woolf was an "unsuccessful propagandist," and that "when she deserted her art for propaganda, as in *Three Guineas*, ... she lost her grasp of reality and ended by *speaking to herself*"[18] (italics mine), although according to her biographer, Quentin Bell, "a great many women wrote to express their enthusiastic approval."[19] Not, it must be noted, Queenie Leavis, in *Scrutiny*, who "denounced Woolf's feminism as dangerous and silly, attacked her ... as not being a real woman because she was not a mother and . . . incapable of being a true socialist because she was not a member of the working class. . . . [She] defended Oxford and Cambridge for excluding women, insisting that most women were not bright enough to deserve an education."[20]

As Carroll says, even when Woolf is not attacked as apolitical, or a hater of the working class, the political content of her work, even her nonfiction, goes unnoticed.[21] How has this extraordinary recategorization taken place? Thanks to Carroll and to Jane Marcus' "Art and Anger" we can now see evidence of how it happened. Although it may be natural that Herbert Marder, a male critic, even when writing about Woolf's feminism, can see that *Mrs. Dalloway* and *To the Lighthouse* convey

"vivid pictures of . . . domestic tyranny" and can yet complain
that they "do not converge on a central 'problem'"[22]—it is surely
uncomfortable for a patriarch to see patriarchy as the central
problem—still, in this case most of the groundwork for the
recategorization was laid by people much closer to Woolf: her
husband and some of her friends. Carroll traces the process as
it occurred after the publication of *Three Guineas:*

> The response of the men of her own circle was cool, uncom-
> prehending, or openly hostile. . . . she wrote in her diary, "I
> didn't get so much praise from L [Leonard] as I hoped." . . .
> Leonard Woolf later . . . referred to it in his autobiography
> *Downhill All the Way* as a "political pamphlet" in the tradition
> of Mary Wollstonecraft, but did not . . . [mention] its con-
> tents. Maynard Keynes "was both angry and contemptuous;
> it was, he declared, a silly argument and not very well writ-
> ten." E. M. Forster thought it "the worst of her books." Quen-
> tin Bell . . . [was uncomprehending] "what really seemed
> wrong was the attempt to involve . . . women's rights with . . .
> the ever-growing menace of Fascism and war. The connec-
> tion between the two questions seemed tenuous."[23]

When E. M. Forster gave the Rede Lecture on Virginia Woolf
after her death, he said that Woolf would not consider improv-
ing the world since the mess was man-made and she, as a
woman, had no responsibility for it, that Woolf's feminism
was "peculiar," and "responsible for the worst of her books—the
cantankerous *Three Guineas* and the less successful streaks in
Orlando." He then stated that Woolf was not a great writer
because she "had no great cause at heart," that she despised the
working class and was "a lady." He adds, "In the 1940s I think she
had not much to complain of and kept on grumbling from

habit." Possibly remembering Woolf's scorn for the state of mind which desires a "highly ornamental" pot from the headmaster ("the private-school stage of human existence") in *A Room of One's Own* (p. 110), he went on to award her "a row of little silver cups" for her novels.[24]

The above performance strongly suggests malice, but it was Leonard Woolf who called his wife "the least political animal since Aristotle invented the definition." As Jane Marcus puts it:

> In the interest, I'm sure, of protecting her reputation, . . . [he] suppressed some of his wife's feminist and socialist writings. In *Collected Essays* he tells us when an essay originally appeared in *TLS* [Times Literary Supplement] but not when one appeared originally in *The Daily Worker*. He reprinted an early draft of Woolf's introduction to Margaret Llewellyn Davies's *Life as We Have Known It* rather than a later version which she reworked with the help of the working women themselves.[25]

Marcus goes on to describe Woolf's "Professions for Women" which "exists in the Berg collection in a version three times as long and three times as strong" as the one Leonard Woolf printed in *The Death of the Moth and Other Essays*. (It is now obtainable in *The Pargiters* [New York: Harcourt Brace Jovanovich, 1978], pp. xxvii–xliv.) Much of Marcus' "Art and Anger" is devoted to the essay; for example, omitted from the printed essay is the following tribute to Dame Ethel Smythe:

> She is of the race of pioneers, of pathmakers. She has gone before and felled trees and blasted rocks . . .

But the version Woolf herself wrote first and then cancelled goes like this:

[She is] one of the icebreakers, the gun runners, the window smashers. The armoured tanks who climbed the rough ground, drew the enemies [*sic*] fire.

The unpublished version of the essay goes on with an astonishing dialogue between "fisherwoman's" reason and imagination, in which the imagination (pulling on her stockings) hears from the reason, "My dear, you were going altogether too far," and with a sketch about "a man returning from a hard day in the city" to find the kitchenmaid reading Plato, the cook writing a Mass in B Flat, the parlormaid playing billiards, and the housemaid doing mathematics.[26] But I am giving into irresistible temptation and stealing from Marcus' splendid essay (which also contains much about Elizabeth Robins, an actress and unjustly ignored novelist, whose books Marcus' article means you to read). Berenice Carroll's equally compelling essay is also a temptation to theft, especially her political interpretations of Woolf's novels, which deal with Woolf's fictional comments on British society, from Peter Walsh, the socialist who loves to see young men marching, to the institutional violence of psychiatry, to the family tyranny of the patriarch, which is—despite Marder's puzzlement and Bell's incomprehension—*the* central issue. Here are some other, still radical, issues with which she deals in *Three Guineas*: the falsity of radical chic and downward mobility (p. 177), the existence and importance of female values (p. 78), free universities (pp. 33–35), the dangers of a male mind-set in women who enter the professions (p. 59), pensions for spinsters (p. 68), the importance of small presses and underground presses (p. 18), wages for parenting and housework (p. 110), the necessity for competition and the resulting exclusively linear hierarchy upon which patriarchy rests (p. 20), and many emphatic statements that the personal is political (e.g., p. 142). Her vocabulary is nontechnical and she speaks of the abstract in concrete terms—like the brilliant novelist she is—which may be one of the reasons the men of her circle disliked the book so much. Although crammed with facts and references, it has the wrong *style*; it is personal and sounds unscholarly, a charge often levelled at modern feminist writing. That is, the tone is not impersonal, detached, and dry enough—in short, not patriarchal enough—to produce belief.

8.
Anomalousness

S HE DIDN'T WRITE IT.
She wrote it, but she shouldn't have.
She wrote it, but look what she wrote about.
She wrote it, but "she" isn't really an artist and "it" isn't really serious, of the right genre—i.e., really art.
She wrote it, but she wrote only one of it.
She wrote it, but it's only interesting/included in the canon for one, limited reason.
She wrote it, but there are very few of her.

Here are some anthologies and academic lists, chosen at random, which may aid in seeing how few of her there are.

The Golden Treasury, edited by F. T. Palgrave in 1861, was re-edited by Oscar Williams in 1961.[1] Palgrave declares his intention to include only lyrics by writers not living in 1855, "lyric" being defined as "some single thought, feeling, or situation." Williams, who has both added poets to the periods Palgrave covers and brought the anthology up to 1955, says that Palgrave's "own definition of the lyrical as unity of feeling or thought" has been kept as a "determinant of choice," although both standards are flexible enough to include, for Palgrave, Shelley's "To a Skylark" and Keats' "Ode to Autumn"; and for Williams, Eliot's "The Journey of the Magi," Auden's "In Memory of W. B. Yeats," and Lindsay's "The Congo." Palgrave includes four women: Anna Letitia Barbauld, Jane Elliott, Lady Anne Lindsay, and Lady Carolina Nairne, all active mainly in the eighteenth century; the latter three were Scotswomen. Each is represented by one selection. Palgrave did not include either Aphra Behn or Anne Finch, Countess of Winchilsea, although some of their works certainly fall within his definition of the lyric. Nor, in his introduction, does he mention the then-famous Elizabeth Barrett Browning as one of the living poets who "will no doubt claim and obtain their place among the best." Emily Brontë (died 1848) is neither mentioned nor included. Palgrave also omitted Donne, Blake, and Traherne, all added by Williams.

In order to count the percentage of women included in this anthology, I have omitted all poets dead before 1650. The assumption that no women dead before 1650 wrote anything at all is questionable (see epilogue), but since it's very probably an assumption Palgrave and Williams would make (as would other anthologists) there's no need to load the figures. It's probably fair to assume that Williams would not include Palgrave's female lyricists but impossible to tell which of the male poets he would likewise delete. I will therefore give both sets of figures: Williams' female choices are 8 percent of the total number of poets in the anthology; the addition of Palgrave's choices raises the total to 11 percent.

Of Williams' fourteen women additions, six are nineteenth-century poets: Emily Bronte, Christina Rossetti, Emily Dickinson, Alice Meynell, Elizabeth Barrett Browning, and (surprisingly) George Eliot. There are no seventeenth- or eighteenth-century additions to Palgrave's four. The remaining eight are twentieth-century figures: Leonie Adams, Elizabeth Bishop, Ruth Herschberger, Esther Matthews, Edna St. Vincent Millay, Marianne Moore, Elinor Wylie, and Gene Derwood. The only women represented by more than two selections apiece are Gene Derwood (seven), Emily Dickinson (eight), and Edna Millay (eleven). Elizabeth Barrett Browning is represented by two of the *Sonnets from the Portuguese*, and Christina Rossetti and Dante Gabriel Rossetti each by two poems. If we compare female poets represented by more than two selections with male poets similarly represented, there are three women out of a total of sixty, or 5 percent. (Only one of these women is not a twentieth-century poet.) To recall Van Gerven, "Since . . . only contemporary women poets are represented in any number, it becomes clear that a woman must be extraordinary to outlive her generation—And that a man need not."[2]

In *A Treasury of Great Poems*, Louis Untermeyer includes Aphra Behn and Anne Finch, Countess of Winchilsea (whom Williams excludes). Untermeyer's twentieth-century choices (except for Millay) differ entirely from Williams', yet he ends up with much the same percentage of women poets as William does (if we subtract Palgrave's choices): 8.6 percent of the total. This figure holds, by the way, either with or without the inclusion of both editors' twentieth-century male and female choices.

In Auden and Pearson's far less idiosyncratic *Poets of the English Language* (which ends with Yeats), 5 percent of the authors listed are women. (Again I have considered 1650 as a rough beginning date.) Anne Bradstreet is present, but Aphra Behn and Elizabeth Barrett Browning are absent, although in evidence are such male figures as John Byrom, Henry Alabaster, and John Wolcot. In all three anthologies there are sections of anonymous ballads, but no speculation that the authors of some of these may have been female, although an Elizabethan scholar, Frederick O. Waage, notes "the strong tendency of all social ballads to vindicate covertly their women."[3] I would certainly hesitate to attribute a later ballad like "Once I wore my apron low" to male authorship, and even among the earlier ones there are some which suggest not only female authorship but female revenge—for example, "May Colvin." (Here the false young man who has drowned six women attempts to drown a seventh, but wants her to take off her clothes, which are too costly to rot in the sea. Pretending modesty, she bids him to turn his back and when he does, throws *him* into the sea, triumphantly telling him to keep company with the women he's drowned.)

To turn again to the graduate reading list of the University of Washington's Department of English (for August 1977) we find no women from 1660 to 1780, four female novelists (but no poets) in nineteenth-century England, and in the United States (up to 1900) four women. The twentieth-century list includes one female novelist, Virginia Woolf, and out of an elective selection of seven novelists, one black man (Ralph Ellison) and one white woman (Doris Lessing). Out of a similar elective selection of eight poets, two are (white) women: Larkin and Rich. Counting again from about 1660, the number of women is about 6 percent. In an earlier list (1968) Chopin, Chesnutt, and Bradstreet do not appear, but Edith Wharton (invisible in 1977) does. In both lists, Cotton Mather appears but not Margaret Fuller; in 1977 Rochester, William Cowper, and William Collins but not Mary Wollstonecraft. Missing also are Aphra Behn, Fanny Burney, Elizabeth Barrett, and Christina Rossetti; and to give my own very partial list of twentieth-century omissions: Willa Cather (Ernest Hemingway is represented by three selections), Dorothy Richardson, Djuna Barnes, Katherine Mansfield, Carson McCullers, Isak Dinesen, Marianne Moore, Zora Neale Hurston, Elizabeth Bishop, and so on and so on.

What is so striking about these examples is that although the percentage of women included remains somewhere between

5 percent and 8 percent, the personnel change rather conspicuously from book to book; Aphra Behn appears and vanishes, Anne Bradstreet is existent or nonexistent according to whom you read, Elizabeth Barrett Browning and Emily Brontë bob up and down like corks, Edith Wharton is part of English literature in 1968 and banished to the outer darkness in 1977—and yet there are always enough women for that 5 percent and never quite enough to get much past 8 percent. It recalls the proportion of female entries (about 7 percent) in those freshman textbooks, chosen not as selections of great literature but in order to teach freshmen to read and write: "the ratio of women writers . . . was fairly constant: about 7%."[4]

In a study of courses given by the Department of English of the women's college she once attended, Elaine Showalter finds (of the writers listed in courses past the freshman year) 17 women out of 313, or just about 5 percent. But which 5 percent? Showalter writes:

> In the twenty-one courses beyond the freshman level . . . there were . . . such [male] luminaries as William Shenstone, James Barrie, and Dion Boucicault; and . . . Lady Mary Wortley Montagu, Anne Bradstreet, Mrs. Centlivre, Fanny Burney, Jane Austen, Charlotte and Emily Brontë, George Eliot, Margaret Fuller, Emily Dickinson, Sarah Orne Jewett, Lady Gregory, Virginia Woolf, Dorothy Richardson, Marianne Moore, Gertrude Stein, and Djuna Barnes.

She adds: "the *Norton Anthology* . . . includes 169 men and 6 women,"[5] 3½ percent and 11.6 percent. Average: 7 percent.

Showalter talks of imbalance, but what bothers me is the constancy of the imbalance despite the changes in personnel. For example, Showalter's English Department includes many more women than the University of Washington list; yet in the former case the percentage of women is lower, not higher, than in the latter. It seems that when women are brought into a reading list, a curriculum, or an anthology, men arrive, too—let the number of men drop and the women mysteriously disappear. Nonetheless, as Van Gerven says:

> the inclusion of only the most extraordinary women [but not only the most extraordinary men] . . . distorts the relevance of those few women . . . who remain. Since women are so often thus isolated in anthologies . . . they seem odd, unconventional, and therefore, a little trivial . . .

She adds:

> When Dickinson, or any woman poet for that matter, is isolated from all writing in her own and succeeding generations, she appears bizarre, extraneous. . . . Since women writers are thus isolated, they often do not fit into the literary historian's "coherent view of the total literary culture." . . . As each succeeding generation of women . . . is excluded from the literary record, the connections between women . . . writers become more and more obscure, which in turn simply justifies the exclusion of more and more women on the grounds that they are anomalous—they just don't fit in.[6]

Pollution of quality via anomalousness is similar to *pollution of agency via abnormality.* Thus R. P. Blackmur, writing of Emily Dickinson, can speak of

> [her] private and eccentric . . . relation to the business of poetry. She was neither a professional poet nor an amateur; she was a private poet who wrote indefatigably as other women cook or knit . . . [driven] to poetry instead of

antimacassars. Neither her personal education nor the habit of her society . . . gave her the least inkling that poetry is a rational and objective art . . .[7]

Thus Dickinson's *anomalousness* as a poet, in part referable to her lack of proper education, leads to an assertion of her personal eccentricity (pollution of agency via abnormality) which along with a recategorizing of Dickinson as not-a-poet and her work as equivalent to antimacassars, converges on the final judgment: her poetry is not what poetry ought to be. Blackmur wrote in 1937, but what he said is not far from the *Commercial Advertiser* review of 1891:

Extreme hunger often causes strange visions. That this hermitess never satisfied, perhaps never could satisfy, her craving for human companionship, may have first brought her into her strangely visionary state. Upon the theme of human love she becomes absurdly, if not blasphemously, intemperate.[8]

Again pollution of agency is given as the reason for the defects in Dickinson's work, nor are the defects very different: she is "driven" and "hungry," *therefore* not "rational" or temperate. In both accounts she appears as totally isolated, a "private" poet or a "hermitess" whose talent came from nowhere and bore no relation to anything. Yet according to other sources this anomalous being can be placed squarely in a public literary tradition, influenced by it and influencing it in turn. Moers writes:

Dickinson had been reading about Mrs. Browning in Kate Field's memorial tribute . . . in the September 1861 *Atlantic Monthly* just as, earlier that year, she had read of Julia Ward Howe's . . . abridgment of George Sand's autobiography. . . .

hundreds of phrases of Dickinson's ... suggest she had the whole of *Aurora Leigh* almost by heart.... Dickinson named Mrs. Browning as mentor; she referred often in her letters to her poems, and to the portraits that friends had sent her.

Moers adds: "Browning scholars do not mention it." And, "Among ... [some] Dickinsonians ... the literary relationship is treated with shocked prurience." (She is referring to John Evangelist Walsh's *The Hidden Life of Emily Dickinson*, published in 1971.) According to Moers, Dickinson read little, despite her "single year ... at Mount Holyoke." She knew Emerson "well ... perhaps a little Thoreau and Hawthorne; but she pretended, at least, not to have read a line of Whitman, no Melville, no Poe, no Irving...." But she read:

and re-read ... Helen Hunt Jackson and Lydia Maria Child, and Harriet Beecher Stowe, and Lady Georgina Fullerton, and Dinah Maria Craik, and Elizabeth Stuart Phelps, and Rebecca Harding Davis, and Harriet Prescott Spofford, and Francesca Alexander, and Mathilda Mackarness and everything that George Eliot ... ever wrote.

Helen Hunt Jackson "correctly valued Emily Dickinson's poetry and urged her to publish."[9]

As for those whom Dickinson influenced, Amy Lowell wrote "Sisters" in 1925, affirming Dickinson as an "older sister."[10] Rich's "I Am in Danger—Sir" calls Dickinson her ancestor.[11] Juhasz, herself a poet, calls Dickinson "the great woman poet to serve as foremother" and goes on to quote from Lowell's "Sisters," Lynn Strongin's "Emily Dickinson Postage Stamp" (1972), and her own "The Poems of Women" (1973).[12] Van Gerven speculates about Dickinson's possible influence on other women poets.[13]

As for other connections between literary women, Moers' *Literary Women* is a mine of cross-references: if Dickinson read Elizabeth Barrett Browning, the latter "had read it all" [fiction by women] and once said that on her tombstone should be written "Ci-gît the greatest novel reader in the world" (p. 61). She corresponded with Harriet Beecher Stowe. Charlotte Brontë went to London, exhibiting "an awkwardness and timidity in literary society that have become legendary"—except with Harriet Martineau (p. 64). George Eliot corresponded with Stowe. Jane Austen read Sarah Harriet Burney, Mrs. Jane West, Anna Maria Porter, Mrs. Anne Grant, Elizabeth Hamilton, Laetitia Matilda Hawkins, Helen Maria Williams, "and the rest of the women writers of her day." She studied Maria Edgeworth and Fanny Burney (pp. 66–67). Nor were all the associations literary. George Eliot knew Barbara Leigh Smith (founder of the Association for Promoting the Employment of Women) (p. 28); Charlotte Brontë knew the feminist Mary Taylor; Mrs. Gaskell knew Bessie Parks and read Mrs. Tonna; Harriet Beecher Stowe wrote the introduction to the 1844 edition of Mrs. Tonna's *Works* (p. 39). George Sand reviewed *Uncle Tom's Cabin* with "All honor and respect to you, Madame Stowe" (p. 55), while George Eliot's famous letter about *Daniel Deronda* and anti-Semitism in England was addressed to Stowe, "whom she honored as her predecessor" (p. 59). Pairings of student with literary mentor are cited by Moers: Willa Cather and Sarah Orne Jewett, Jean Rhys and Charlotte Brontë, Carson McCullers and Isak Dinesen, Nathalie Sarraute and Ivy Compton-Burnett (p. 68). Elizabeth Barrett and Miss Mitford were correspondents (Flush was a gift from Mitford to her friend), and both wished to send their books, "tied together in a parcel for courage to the great Madame Sand." Miss Barrett wrote, "I would give anything to have a letter from her, though it smelt of cigar. And it would, of course!" (pp. 82–83). Mrs. Browning later visited Mme. Sand twice, despite her husband's objections. There are

other surprising influences Moers finds: George Eliot on Ger-
trude Stein, for example (pp. 98–99). As for single novels, *Con-
suelo* was read by Charlotte Brontë, Mary Taylor said it was worth
learning French to read it, and Willa Cather kept Sand's portrait
over her mantelpiece into the 1930s (p. 289). (Moers does not
mention along with George Eliot's *Armgart* Isak Dinesen's Pel-
legrina Leoni, but there may be a connection there, too.) Moers
also traces the enormous influence of Mrs. Radcliffe (her books
turn up, among other places, in *Shirley*—pp. 192–193) and the
even greater influence of *Corinne* (which turns up everywhere).
She also finds, in women's works, repeated themes which a syn-
opsis could only travesty.

In some other places studies are beginning to be made of the
connections between women artists. For example, Virginia Woolf
knew that Geraldine Jewsbury knew Jane Carlyle, but her essay
on the two of them gives the impression that Jewsbury was otherwise isolated.[14] A recent issue of *Heresies*, however, links as "inti-
mates" Geraldine Jewsbury, Charlotte Cushman, Fanny Kemble,
Harriet Hosmer, and several other women artists. There is the
circle around Natalie Barney in the twenties. (Barney complains
vigorously of the "artificial Renée [Vivien] whom Colette presents in *Ces Plaisirs!*")[15] Nor are all these networks among artists;
Blanche Weisen Cook documents the female support groups
surrounding the married Crystal Eastman (who, "surrounded
by men who shared her work" had "a feminist support group
as well"), and the homosexual Jane Addams and Lillian Wald,
"involved almost exclusively with women." She also describes the
extent to which these relationships between women, whether
sexual or not, have been ignored by historians. When the relationships are homosexual (as in the case of Mount Holyoke president Mary E. Woolley, who lived for years with her lover, the
chairwoman of the English Department), it is understandable
that "the historical evidence was juggled." Cook provides some

examples of the astounding lengths to which historians will go to explain away the obvious.[16] But surely Emily Dickinson's admiration for Elizabeth Barrett is not socially tabooed. Yet Moers can observe, "Among most Dickinsonians the literary relationship is treated with embarrassment" and "Browning scholars . . . do not mention it." And elsewhere:

> Scholarship has averted its refined and weary eyes from the female fiction that Austen's letters inform us was her daily sustenance in the years she became one of the greatest writers in the language.

And again Moers complains that the "stability and integrity" of Mrs. Radcliffe's Gothic heroines have been made to vanish from modern view by

> what was done with the figure by the male writers who followed Mrs. Radcliffe. For most of them . . . the Gothic heroine was quintessentially a defenseless victim, a weakling . . . whose sufferings are the source of her erotic fascination. [Moers suggests elsewhere that the proper model for Emily in *The Mysteries of Udolpho* is not de Sade's female victims but Katharine Hepburn in *The African Queen*.][17]

From Dolores Palomo I find also that the refined eyes of scholarship condemn "one-half to two-thirds of the fiction printed in the eighteenth century" as minor, mediocre, or salacious—that is, the fiction written by women.[18]

Thus the female tradition in literature has been either ignored, derided, or even (as with Mrs. Radcliffe's property-minded heroines) taken over and replaced. Why? Here is one possible answer, not aesthetic but political (by Judith Long Laws, a psychologist):

Tokenism is ... found whenever a dominant group is under pressure to share privilege, power, or other desirable commodities with a group which is excluded. . . . tokenism advertises a promise of mobility which is severely restricted in quantity. . . . the Token does not become assimilated into the dominant group, but is destined for permanent marginality...[19]

Here is another: Novelist Samuel Delany has argued that outside of specifically social situations (like cocktail parties), Americans are trained to "see" a group in which men predominate to the extent of 65 percent to 75 percent as half male and half female. In business and on the street, groups in which women actually number 50 percent tend to be seen as being *more* than 50 percent female.[20] It is not impossible that some similar, unconscious mechanism controls the number of female writers which looks "proper" or "enough" to anthologists and editors. (I am reminded of the folk wisdom of female academics, one of whom whispered to me before a meeting at which we were the only women present, "Don't sit next to me or they'll say we're taking over.")

There are three elements here: a promise, numerical restrictions, and permanent marginality. We have seen the restrictions on the quantity of visibility allowed women writers: that 5 to 8 percent representation. Quality can be controlled by denial of agency, pollution of agency, and false categorizing. I believe that the *anomalousness* of the woman writer—produced by the double standard of content and the writer's isolation from the female tradition—is the final means of ensuring permanent marginality. In order to have her "belong" fully to English literature, the tradition to which she belongs must also be admitted. Other writers must be admitted along with their tradition, written and unwritten. Speech must be admitted. Canons of excellence and conceptions of excellence must change, perhaps beyond recognition. In short, we have a complete collapse of the original solution to the problem of the "wrong" people creating the "right" values. When this happens, the very idea that some people *are* "wrong" begins to fade. And that makes it necessary to recognize what has been done to the "wrong" people and why. And that means recognizing one's own complicity in an appalling situation. It means anger, horror, helplessness, fear for one's own privilege, a conviction of personal guilt and what for professional intellectuals may be even worse, a conviction of one's own profound stupidity. It may mean fear of retaliation. It means knowing that *they* are watching *you*. Imagine a middle-aged, white, male professor (the typical sort in the profession) asked to let into the Sacred Canon of Literature the following:

> call me
> roach and presumptuous
> nightmare on your white pillow . . .

> AUDRE LORDE, "The Brown Menace or Poem
> to the Survival of Roaches"[21]

Anger is hard to take. But there are worse things. Imagine our professor confronted with a long, elegant, comic poem about impotence, masturbation, and premature ejaculation. Here is Canto 9:

> In vain th' inraged Youth essay'd
> To call its [his penis'] fleeting vigor back.
> No motion 'twill from Motion take;
> Excess of Love his Love betray'd:
> In vain he Toils, in vain Commands;
> The Insensible fell weeping in his Hand.[22]

The above is from Aphra Behn's "The Disappointment." Of those who are not ignored completely, dismissed as writing about the "wrong" things, condemned for (whatever passes for) impropriety (that year), described as of merely technical interest (on the basis of a carefully selected few worst works), falsely categorized as other than artists, condemned for writing in the wrong genre, or out of genre, or simply joked about, or blamed for what has, in fact, been deleted from or misinterpreted out of their work by others, it is still possible to say, quite sincerely:

She wrote it, but she doesn't fit in.

Or, more generously: *She's wonderful, but where on earth did she come from?*

9.
Lack of Models

MODELS AS GUIDES to action and as indications of possibility are important to all artists—indeed to all people—but to aspiring women artists they are doubly valuable. In the face of continual and massive discouragement, women need models not only to see in what ways the literary imagination has (as Moers says) been at work on the fact of being female, but also as assurances that they can produce art without inevitably being second-rate or running mad or doing without love. It is here that the false categorizing of artists into whores, sad spinsters, devoted submissive wives, and (recently) tragic suicides converges with the obliteration of the female tradition in literature to work the greatest harm.

It deprives the young of models.

At first glance, the lack of models and the assertion that there is a female tradition in literature seem contradictory. I think not.

One difference is in the age of the women involved—female support groups exist but they must be created anew by each generation, so that what was missing during one's formative years may (with luck and drive) be built or discovered later on at a considerable cost in time, energy, and self-confidence. I also suspect that higher education has had one bad effect not foreseen in the middle of the last century: an informal acquaintance with the common female tradition in literature has been replaced by a formal education which entirely omits it. In the former case the models and the tradition, though denigrated, were there. In the latter case all but a few anomalous women have become invisible. Thus Elaine Showalter writes:

> Let us imagine a woman student entering college to major in English literature. In her freshman year . . . the texts in her course would be selected for their timeliness, or their relevance or their power to involve the reader. . . . any of the [recently advertised] . . . texts . . . for Freshman English . . . [like] *The Responsible Man*, "for the student who wants literature relevant to the world in which he lives," or *Conditions of Men*, or *Man in Crisis: Perspectives on the Individual and His World*, or . . . *Representative Men: Cult Heroes of Our Time*, in which the thirty-three men represent such categories of heroism as the writer, the poet, the dramatist, the artist, and the guru . . . the only women included are the Actress Elizabeth Taylor and the Existential Heroine Jacqueline Onassis.
>
> Perhaps the student would read a collection of stories like *The Young Man in American Literature: The Initiation Theme*, or sociological literature like *The Black Man and the Promise of America* . . . [or] she might study the eternally relevant classics, such as *Oedipus*; as a professor remarked in a recent issue of *College English*, all of us want to kill our fathers and

marry our mothers. And . . . she would inevitably arrive at the favorite book of all Freshman English courses, the classic of adolescent rebellion, *Portrait of the Artist as a Young Man*.[1]

It's not surprising, given the above, that Florence Howe can note (in the same issue of the same journal):

My women students consistently consider women writers (and hence themselves, though that is not said outright) inferior to men. . . . [I have had] admissions from many . . . that they secretly want to write, that they should like to have "ideas" and "imagination," but that they feel it's too late for them.[2]

Let me again quote Marilyn Hacker, teaching in the fall of 1976:

. . . in *The New Republic* . . . a capsule review of Poetry Books Published in 1976. He [Harold Bloom] didn't mention *one* book by a woman . . . in a cassette catalogue I received (in my professional capacity) . . . in the poetry section, out of 60 titles, lectures on Dickinson, Moore, Louise Bogan, and Plath [8% of the total, again], all given by men. In the novel, *nothing!*[3]

In this relative absence of female literary models, female teachers might serve as encouragement to some students, if not specifically in the arts, then at least in the realm of high culture in general. Certainly the feminism of the last ten years can be expected to result in an increase in the number of women in college and university classrooms and an increase in the percentage of such women found in the higher ranks. Yet in June of 1978 *On Campus with Women* gave the following figures:

> In the academic year 1974–75, the percentage of women faculty was 22.5%. In 1975–76 this dropped to 21% ... by 1976–77 the percentage had risen ... to 22.4%.... In 1976 a third of the female faculty were in the upper two ranks [7.4% of the total faculty, a figure eerily similar to that for female representation in course curricula, anthologies, etc.]. In 1977, only 28% ... The comparable figures for males are 63% in 1976 and 62% in 1977.[4]

If there are relatively few female models to imitate in higher education or in literature, why do some women become writers anyway? Is it possible they had access to models most students knew nothing about? For three contemporary writers, at least, that seems not to be true. Here is poet Erica Jong, describing her literary education:

> being a woman means, unfortunately, believing a lot of male definitions. . . . I had learned what an orgasm was from D. H. Lawrence, disguised as Lady Chatterley.... (For years I measured my orgasms against Lady Chatterley's and wondered what was wrong with me. . . .) I learned from Dostoyevski that they [women] have no religious feeling. I learned from Swift and Pope that they have too much religious feeling (and therefore can never be quite rational). I learned from Faulkner that they are earth-mothers and at one with the moon and the tide and the crops. I learned from Freud that they have deficient superegos and are forever "incomplete."

Jong goes on to say "poetry for me was a masculine noun" possibly because of the

> visiting writer [who] went on and on about how women *couldn't possibly* be authors. Their experience was too limited. . . . They didn't know blood and guts and fucking whores and puking in the streets. . . . this . . . made me miserable.[5]

Adrienne Rich, who speaks elsewhere not of the "Tarzan crossed with King Kong" model of art Jong describes, but of a more subtle desire to write as men do (since that is the acceptable model) also comments on the lack of a female tradition:

> Dickinson's work wasn't available in a complete, unbowdlerized edition until the Fifties. . . . [In my college days we] knew H. D., if at all, as the author of a few gemlike Imagist lyrics. But in her long, late poems . . . she was reaching out beyond the disintegration . . . beyond the destruction of World War II, to say "we women/poets . . . will leave the ruins and seek something else." . . . She was seeking . . . for myths of the female, creating female heroes, a female divine presence, and claiming her vision as a woman poet. None of this was known to me then.[6]

None of this was known to me then. Aspirants without predecessors or with predecessors tainted in one way or another, what could we do? I remember, as a first-year student, being asked cheerfully by my graduate student date how I, an aspiring novelist, could reconcile my ambition to write with the "fact" that no woman had ever produced "great literature." How could I answer? I "knew" that Virginia Woolf was limited and ladylike ("tragedy at the tea-party" was my date's generous phrase), Charlotte Brontë was minor, *Wuthering Heights* "unrealistic" (the "self-consistent monster" again), and Emily Dickinson a fey spinster who wrote strange little poems of interest only to a few obsessed professors who couldn't explain her technique anyway, because she had none but wrote "intuitively." This odd idea, once applied to the native wood-notes wild of a barbarous Shakespeare (the assumption that artists-of-the-wrong-group create intuitively, not intelligently), crops up all over the place. Louis Untermeyer says that Christina Rossetti's verse "defies analysis,"[7] an idea he may have picked up from Sir Walter Raleigh (the early twentieth-century one) who is quoted *anent* Rossetti thus: "You cannot lecture on really pure poetry any more than you can talk about the ingredients of pure water—it is adulterated, methylated, sanded poetry that makes the best lectures. The only thing that Christina makes me want to do, is cry, not lecture."[8] This kind of romanticizing is a form of the denial of agency, and in conjunction with distinctions of race, class, and sex can be extremely mischievous. The idea that any art is achieved "intuitively" is a dehumanization of the brains, effort, and the traditions of the artist, and a classification of said artist as subhuman. It is those supposed incapable of intelligence, training, or connection with a tradition who are described as working by instinct or intuition. Thus "Negro spirituals" can be enjoyed without being respected, as Untermeyer does. Even Woolf can say of Rossetti: "You were an instinctive poet" and "her verses seemed to have formed themselves whole and entire in her head."[9] With Mozart, this kind of creation means the facility and ease of a genius; with Rossetti it becomes a kind of intuition.

(An extremely vicious recent example of the above in popular culture was an episode ["Renewal"] in the liberal television series *Lou Grant*, broadcast January 30, 1978, and again on June 19, 1978. The story was about an elderly, self-taught, black artist whose murals were characterized as "primitive," "emotional," and motivated by personal loss rather than artistic impulse. Few recent examples of racism on television can have been as bad as the white characters' loving gazes, suffused with tender, protective indulgence, as they watched the painter's wide-eyed, dumb naïveté [at one point much was made of his mispronunciation of "chiaroscuro"]. The play assumed that the appealing stupidity displayed by this adult artist was real [not a form of shuffling] and that sentimental condescension was a virtuous and appropriate white response.)

So what did I say, confronted by the "fact" of female inferiority?

I said, "I'll be the first." Three years later, one of the few women in a college writing class (at the time, I didn't wonder why there were so few of us), I submitted for class discussion part of a novel I was writing; it was about the comic sufferings of wallflowers at a high school dance. The class dismissed it: yes, it was funny but everyone knew about high school dances; they weren't important subjects. A male classmate's chapter of a novel drew, on the contrary, deep respect; here was writing that was raw, powerful, elemental, and true. His piece about picking up a (totally mute) whore, a fight in a bar, and then (in the subplot) a husband of indeterminate character having painful intercourse on the kitchen floor with a wife, just out of the hospital for the excision of a coccyxal cyst, who stank. Terminal sentence: "That night their idiot child was conceived." Although my female friend and I went outside after class and laughed ourselves silly, I still began to wonder whether I had the proper kind of experience to be a writer. The class judgment had been clearly in terms of content. Mine wouldn't do.

Luckily I wasn't told that my style wouldn't do. Here is Cynthia Ozick, however, teaching in the mid-sixties. Her students, reading Flannery O'Connor's *Wise Blood*, hear O'Connor referred to (after three weeks) as "she"; there is instant astonishment except for one student, "intelligent and Experimental, one of my rare literates, herself an anomaly because she was enrolled in the overwhelmingly male College of Engineering." This student insists:

"But I could *tell* she was a woman. . . . Her sentences are a woman's sentences." I asked her what she meant and how she could tell. "Because they're sentimental," she said; "they're not concrete like a man's." I pointed out whole paragraphs, pages even, of unsentimental, so-called tough prose. "But she *sounds* like a woman—she has to sound that way because she is," said the future engineer.[10]

Well, this is not 1966 or thereabouts (Ozick's experience) or 1956 (mine) and students no longer learn about Mary Wollstonecraft, for example, from Lundberg and Farnham's *Modern Woman: The Lost Sex*,[11] where in 1953 I had the misfortune to meet her—or rather, Lundberg and Farnham's caricature of her, who suffers from every neurosis possible (except courage). (Kate Millett discusses the book briefly in *Sexual Politics*, calling it of "enormous influence both on the general public and . . . in the academic curriculum.")[12] According to Lundberg and Farnham, the women's movement "stood on a bedrock foundation of hatred" (p. 33) and was "an expression of emotional sickness, of neurosis . . . at its core a deep illness" (p. 143). John Stuart Mill is passive-feminine (p. 193) and Karl Marx's theory is accounted for by "unconscious hatred of parental authority" (p. 31). Nor are forgotten feminists rediscovered solely for the purpose of reviling them, as Lundberg and Farnham did with Wollstonecraft. In "Art and Anger," Jane Marcus raises Elizabeth Robins from oblivion to praise her, but one of the most disheartening things in Robins' career is Robins' own appreciation of the obliteration of women from history, whether feminist or not:

She was appalled at the depth of oblivion that over-
shadowed . . . the women of her generation. She and Mrs.
Humphrey Ward had been arch-enemies over the suffrage
question. Mrs. Ward . . . had made her home a conservative
salon . . . [for] the politicians, intellectuals, and writers
whom she had encouraged. Dead, she was not mourned
by any of them. . . . The same was true of Edith Wharton;
Robins saw that a lifetime of friendship had only inspired
in James "a certain worried desire to do his duty." . . . James
and Shaw had been Elizabeth Robins' champions when she
was the champion of Ibsen. When she herself began to
write, they were silent.[13]

When the memory of one's predecessors is buried, the
assumption persists that there were none and each generation
of women believes itself to be faced with the burden of doing
everything for the first time. And if no one ever did it before, if
no woman was ever that socially sacred creature, "a great writer,"
why do we think we can succeed now? The specter of "If women
can, why haven't they?" is as potent as it was in Margaret Cavendish's time. A (possibly) genuine singularity has become a manufactured one and still has the power to discourage. For example, in A Room of One's Own, Woolf writes of her fictitious novelist,
Mary Carmichael: "She will be a poet . . . in another hundred
years' time."[14]

A hundred years' time? Good heavens (we might Woolfianly
write), is it possible that this snobbish member of the upper
classes, too introverted to leave her study, a believer in no great
cause, bound by the limitations of being a lady (we have E. M.
Forster's word for it) was too lazy or too uneducated to know
that her poet had already occurred—not one hundred years in
the future but sixty-odd years in the past? Can it be that Virginia
Woolf, that omnivorous reader who read old diaries and wrote

about people nobody ever heard of (like Miss Pilkington and Miss Ormerod) *never read Emily Dickinson?* Probably she did not, for *A Room of One's Own* was published in 1929. The first comprehensive collection of Dickinson's work, heavily edited and extensively bowdlerized, was published in 1914 by a relative, Martha Dickinson Bianchi. The more complete *Bolts of Melody* appeared after Woolf's death, in 1945; the complete, unbowdlerized, collected poems did not appear until 1955. Nor are the rediscoveries and reevaluations anything but begun. As late as 1971, the feminist art historian, Linda Nochlin, could write:

The fact of the matter is that there have been no great woman artists as far as we know—although there have been many interesting and good ones. . . . The fact is that there *are* no women equivalents for Michelangelo or Rembrandt, Delacroix or Cézanne, Picasso, or Matisse, or even . . . de Kooning or Warhol.[15]

This is a sticky statement, first in its odd repetition of the word "fact" twice in an area ("great" or "not great") that is clearly a matter of judgment. Second, there is the statement "no great woman artists" in a century that has produced Georgia O'Keeffe, Käthe Kollwitz, and Emily Carr, to name only those *I* happen to like. Third, there is the sliding of "great" into "equivalent"—why should there be? surely one Picasso is enough for any reasonable generation!—and when she adds de Kooning and Warhol to those equivalents, I, for one, am tempted to add "thank God." And why is the list so biased in favor of a certain canon of abstraction—where is Goya, for example?—but this discussion calls for a whole book. Here is a statement, again by a feminist, that is plainly untrue:

Until the twentieth century there was no body of poetry by women in English.[16]

This is Suzanne Juhasz, one year before the publication of Moers' *Literary Women*. Seven years before *Literary Women* we find Mary Ellmann, the originator of the phrase "phallic criticism," herself indulging in exactly what she deplores. For example, in *Thinking about Women* we find her denigrating Charlotte Brontë's supposed rebelliousness as "the appropriation of a modest and utilitarian Byronism by the woman writer" (p. 213). (Compare Kate Millett's appraisal of *Villette*: a meditation on a jail break, a book "too subversive" to be popular.) Thus, although women can write, they must not write angrily. Nor is Ellmann willing to admit that women can—or should—write in what she considers a "masculine" way; at least there is no other way I can explain her intense dislike of Willa Cather. Ellmann speaks of Cather's "bluff, middy-blouse suspicions of . . . sexuality" (p. 114), calls her Nebraska wives "ideal men-in-women," insists upon the masculinity of Ántonia: "she wears men's clothes and conducts her first pregnancy and delivery as a Roman general would" (p. 192). (As I recall *My Ántonia*, the Roman pregnancy appears to be Ellmann's invention.) When we get to Claude Wheeler in *One of Ours* (a refugee from the same small-town narrowness Sherwood Anderson and Sinclair Lewis describe) and find that he is "admired" by Cather because he "aspires to the feminine in spirit" (p. 192), it's hard to know who is employing sexual stereotypes against whom. I believe that Ellmann is made uneasy by Brontë because direct expression of female anger makes her uneasy (the anger in her own book is disguised by irony and mockery, some of it as serpentine as Alice's flamingo), and dislikes Cather because Ellmann herself still believes in certain very old sexual stereotypes: that women cannot write well outside certain limits ("mannishly") and that they lay themselves open to ridicule or male retaliation if they try. I also believe homophobia to have been at work here.

Without models, it's hard to work; without a context, difficult to evaluate; without peers, nearly impossible to speak. Hence the apologetic current of fun Woolf keeps up at Elizabeth Barrett's expense in the essay "Aurora Leigh," and her deriving defects in the poem from defects in the poet's life, a procedure we have seen before. For although Woolf finally speaks of her "ardour and abundance, her brilliant descriptive powers, her shrewd and caustic humor," it's only after mentioning her "bad taste . . . tortured ingenuity, her floundering, scrambling, and confused impetuosity" *because* once let out of her prison, "she was too weak to stand the shock." Woolf goes on: "the novel-poem is not *therefore* the masterpiece that it might have been" (italics mine). But just as the description of the life precedes the literary judgment in this essay, so the description of the reputation precedes Woolf's judgment: "fate has not been kind to Mrs. Browning as a writer. Nobody reads her, nobody discusses her," but the reputation is in turn preceded by something else: the romance, "Passionate lovers in curls and side whiskers."[17] Thus Woolf's novelist's arrangement of materials contradicts her logical argument; if we follow the argument, we find that Elizabeth Barrett is a flawed writer *because* her life was limited. Her bad reputation is *therefore* deserved, although her popular value as the heroine of a romance is charming and *appropriate*. But if this is Woolf's argument, why not start with Woolf's literary judgment, and proceed straightforwardly through the logical stages of the argument (as above)? Instead everything is backwards and the chronological arrangement of the materials tells us that:

1. Elizabeth Barrett's popular value as the heroine of a romance is charming and appropriate.
2. Her reputation as an artist is bad.

3. Her life is limited.
4. Her work is bad.
5. But really her work is pretty good (a surprising jump, here!).

Reverse the causal signs of the argument to accord with the chronological/associational progression of the essay and we have: *Because* Elizabeth Barrett is a valuable popular heroine of romance, *therefore* the limitations of her life are used to justify the limitations that are *therefore* perceived in her work; but I (Woolf, the novelist) cannot help liking her work; *therefore* it is good.

The above is (as I perceive it) the feminist essay Woolf (almost) wrote: a familiar example of recategorizing, like *Wuthering Heights'* transformation from a powerful, realistic novel by a writer to a fantasy by a lonely spinster.

Deprived of tradition, accused of everything from impropriety to ridiculousness to abnormality, assured at best of unlovableness, misery, madness and (lately) suicide, criticized for being feminine, criticized for not being feminine, working with the wrong experiences if their content is recognizably female, "Mandarin" or imitative if it isn't, doomed in any event to second-rateness or (at best) anomalousness, women still go on writing.

But how can they? How do they?

10.
Responses

A
LTHOUGH WOMEN WROTE one-half to two-thirds of the novels published in English in the eighteenth century,[1] and women dominate certain fields such as the detective story or the modern Gothic (in popularity if not in numbers), undoubtedly one response to *Women can't write* is not to. Figures are hard to come by, but in several contemporary professional associations of writers women are certainly underrepresented. In 1974 the female membership of the Science Fiction Writers of America was 18 percent, by my computation; that of the Mystery Writers of America was 23 percent. In summer writing workshops I've attended in science fiction, women have averaged 20 percent or fewer of the total number of students. I've been told, however, that in nonspecialized summer writing conferences women often predominate. Figures for *Books in Print* and similar sources would be interesting, but as far as I know, no one has done the research. I have no figures for the Writer's

Guild. Jeffrey Smith, editor of *Khatru*, maintains that over half the modern Gothics written are by men; however, here, as in the detective story, the most popular authors are women.[2]

Another response is to write, but to agree with the assertion that women's writing must be inferior to men's or that women are (or ought to be) not writers but something else first, for example dutiful wives and mothers. These positions are easier to maintain as a critic than as an artist; thus Elizabeth Hardwick in her capacity as critic could admit to female inferiority without visible pain or protest and even with some *schadenfreude*:

> It is only the whimsical, the cantankerous, the eccentric . . . who would say that any literary work by a woman, marvelous as these may be, is on a level with the very greatest accomplishments of men.

The reason for this is:

> No comradely socialist legislation on women's behalf could accomplish . . . what a bit more muscle tissue, gratuitously offered by nature, might do. . . . not . . . that muscles write books, but . . . *talent and experience being equal*, they may be considered a bit of an advantage. In the end, *it is in the matter of experience that women's disadvantage is catastrophic*. It is very difficult to know how this may be extraordinarily altered.[3] [italics mine]

If the above is ambiguous, consider Hardwick's review of *The Second Sex* on its first appearance in English (comment by Elaine Reuben):

> de Beauvoir, in spite of her absorbing turn of phrase, miraculously does *not* give to me, at least, the impression of being a

masochist, a Lesbian, a termagant, or a man-hater, and . . . this book is not the "self-pitying cry of one who resents being born a woman," as one American housewife-reviewer said. [The italics are Elaine Reuben's, who adds in a footnote, "The ambivalence of *this* review would require a study in itself."][4]

If Hardwick is not in pain in the above (partly, I think because the open admission of inferiority can earn one praise for honesty, and partly because she can thus disassociate herself from even more inferior women), Rebecca Harding Davis is. Accepting as "her ordained situation" that it was her husband "who should be enabled to do his best work," while her obligation "was to help him" she became "a professional workhorse in the field of letters," according to Tillie Olsen. In her biographical essay on Davis, appended to *Life in the Iron Mills*, Olsen goes on to document Davis' tragic conflict *via* Davis' own fiction: for example, *Earthen Pitchers*, a serial published in *Scribner's Monthly* during 1873–1874. The heroine, a musician, training herself rigorously from child-hood, describes herself thus: "Music is all there is of me." Finding that love is part of her, too, she marries; then her musical career must go. At the end of the story, in a walk by the seashore, nature seems to be reproaching her for the abandonment of her art:

> It seemed to her that she must answer. . . . She began to sing, she knew not what. But the tones were discordant, the voice was cracked. . . . [Her husband joins her] dully conscious that she had been troubled. . . . "You're not really sorry that you leave nothing to the world but that little song?" . . . "I leave my child."
>
> Her husband, at least, was sure she made no moan over that which might have been and was not.

Olsen adds:

In . . . ten years [Davis] had lost her place in the literary world. She no longer published in the *Atlantic*. . . . She no longer believed in, acted upon, the possibility of high achievement for herself. It was the price for children, home, love.[5]

Giving in is one way. Another strategy is to deny some part of the statement *Women can't write*. Faced with the more general statement of female intellectual inferiority, Simone Weil

considered it a great misfortune to have been born female so she had decided to reduce this obstacle as much as possible by simply disregarding it. . . . She was determined to be a man as much as possible.

Weil says of her adolescence:

I seriously thought of dying because of [my] mediocrity. . . . The exceptional gifts of my brother brought my inferiority home to me.

(This mediocre being, who signed her letters to her family "your respectful son," later finished first in her class at the Sorbonne in philosophy.)[6]

Thus it is possible to answer *Women can't create* with *I'm not a woman*. To assert this literally (as the adolescent Weil did) is not kindly treated socially; however, it's possible to recategorize oneself in less obvious ways. One such ploy, according to Marcus, is "the kind of nonthreatening female art which is 'beautifully mandarin or minor' . . . [a] form of indirect discourse which Hortense Calisher calls 'mental hysterectomy.'"[7] Juhasz's analysis of Marianne Moore's poetry, with its images of armored animals, its genderlessness, its seeming impersonality, and its constant self-defense, sees these characteristics as a way of being a woman and a poet without ever (dangerously) putting the two together, and thus an extremely skillful and subtle way of claiming *I'm not a woman*. Juhasz comments:

> [Moore's] feminine virtues of "deference" and "modesty" and charm were the ones with which men are most comfortable (and flattered); while in opting for nonsexuality, she escaped those feminine characteristics that threaten, especially in a woman who also claims—through intelligence and talent—to be an equal. . . . Chastity is non-engagement; it leaves one in a position of safety.[8]

If it is possible to claim that one is not a woman, it's also possible to ignore the problem of the prohibition itself. Thus Mary Ellmann, after more than two hundred pages condemning sexual stereotyping, says that the whole business is something one ought to ignore. While understanding the woman novelist's "compulsion to 'answer' or at least mull over the same oppressive questions" (about women's nature and women's talent) and joining female and black writers as "people looking for their own bodies under razed buildings," she nonetheless concludes, "It is possible for non-fighters neither to referee nor to take fighting seriously. . . . Once the rule of courage is expended, admirable exceptions of cowardice are released."[9]

In one sense Ellmann's advice is impossible—how can you flee a fight that follows you?—but in another sense it is advice many women have followed: *Get out of the "major" genres and into the "minor" ones. Stay on the periphery of culture.* Jane Austen, for example, worked (as some critics tend to forget) in a genre that had been dominated by women for a century *and* one that was looked down upon as trash, a position that may have given her considerable artistic freedom. In 1970 a female honors student of mine wrote an essay on Charlotte Brontë in which "Charlotte's" personal psychopathology and infantile rebellion were compared with "Jane's" cheerful acceptance of society. In August of 1928 female novelists were still being advised gracefully to acknowledge "the limitations of their sex" with Austen as the shining example.[10] That Austen's sunny conformity may have been due to a secure, though small, income and an exceptionally supportive family never occurred to my student—nor that it might be an illusion; after all, we have Brontë's personal papers, but not Austen's. And if we look at Austen's own work we find the following vigorous complaint in her own novel, *Northanger Abbey*:

> I will not adopt that ungenerous and impolitic custom so common with novel writers, of degrading by their contemptuous censure the very performances to the number of which they are themselves adding . . . scarcely ever permitting them to be read by their own heroine, who, if she accidentally take up a novel, is sure to turn over its insipid pages with disgust. . . . Let us not desert one another; we are an injured body. Although our productions have afforded more extensive and unaffected pleasure than any other literary corporation in this world, no species of composition has been so much decried. . . . There seems almost a general wish of decrying the capacity and under-valuing the labour of the novelist, and of slighting the performances which have only genius, wit, and taste to recommend them.[11]

The passage continues for as many lines again. Austen even gets angry enough to compare "novels" with "the Spectator," the matter of which she describes as disgusting, improbable, unnatural, and coarse. This is strong language; "looked down upon as trash" is no exaggeration, according to Austen, who uses the word herself ("the trash with which the press now groans"). I think it no accident that (for example) female choreographers of note were invisible in ballet until the advent of Twyla Tharp (whose dance vocabulary almost amounts to a different art), while women dominated modern dance from its inception. Nor that film criticism (compared with theater criticism) developed a female figure as important as Pauline Kael—until very recently "movies" weren't important. (Mary McCarthy got her first job in theater criticism because the theater wasn't important to the journal that had hired her.) If you are a woman and wish to become preeminent in a field, it's a good idea to (a) invent it and (b) locate it in an area either so badly paid or of such low status that men don't want it; hence Florence Nightingale and Jane Addams. (Both nursing and social work have remained women's work and badly paid, at least in the lower ranks.) Aphra Behn's direct attack on the "wretched fop" who attacked her play, before having seen it, on the grounds that it was a woman's, combines direct attack on the presumption of female inferiority ("waiving the examination why women having equal education with men, were not as capable of knowledge") with the observation that theater is on the periphery of culture and therefore accessible to women:

> Plays have no great room for that which is men's advantage over women, that is learning: we all well know that the immortal Shakespeare's plays (who was not guilty of much more of this than often falls to women's share) have better pleased the world than Jonson's works, though by the way 'tis said that Benjamin was no such rabbi, neither.[12]

Those women who can't (or won't) remain on the periphery of culture can employ other defenses; often they assert that they are exceptional women. Margaret Cavendish's answer to the singularity of her position as an aspirant to literary greatness was the same as mine in 1953, "I'll be the first." In her introduction to one of her treaties on natural philosophy, she writes optimistically:

> I am . . . as ever any of my Sex was, is, or can be; which makes, that although I cannot be Henry the Fifth or Charles the Second, yet I endeavour to be Margaret the First.[13]

Anaïs Nin's tactic, obviously an answer to the charge of abnormality, was to perceive her writing as both new in genre and exclusively feminine:

> I must continue the diary because it is a feminine activity, it is a personal and personified creation, the opposite of the masculine alchemy.[14]

Often even women who did not declare themselves exceptional in print created for themselves a romantic and exotic persona that countered *Women can't create* with *I am more than a woman*—exactly what Lowell asserted about Plath. A contemporary visual artist remembers this technique as it was used by two well-known artists:

> Louise Nevelson . . . made herself into some kind of witch/ sibyl. She isolated herself by the costume. Martha Graham did the same thing.[15]

Edith Sitwell's costume produces the same kind of public image, as do Marianne Moore's cloak and tri-cornered hat. (I remember seeing her walking on the Promenade in Brooklyn Heights some time in 1960 or 1961. She looked fierce, independent, admirable, wind-ruffled, and somewhat resentful—possibly because I was staring at her. I was too shy to attempt any kind of conversation.) What is appealed to as metaphor in one culture can give legitimacy in literal terms in another. Thus an essay in *Heresies* discusses a woman artist who, in her culture, is also exceptional:

> Abatan is a woman artist of stature among the Egbado Yoruba. She is not an ordinary woman; she has religio-political and economic status. But had she not been born the daughter of a potter and not come into the world through the grace of [the deity] Eyinle and not been talented, she would not have had the opportunity to make figurative pots and accrue status. This safeguards the making of figurative images from incursion by just any woman.[16]

The techniques described so far are ways of coping with the various forms taken by *Women can't write*, but they are not in direct conflict with the statement itself. In various ways they redefine the terms "women" and "write"; thus Nin, in effect, recategorizes "write" (in a way I find false), as the others, in one way or another, recategorize "women" into *all except me*. Some writers attack the statement directly. One of these attacks, which focuses on the content of women's writing, might be called an appeal to truth.

Women can write because they can see truths that others [male writers] *can't*. This is similar to the defense of realism in the nineteenth century, although the nineteenth-century realists, Zola for example, were not defending themselves against charges of sexual incapacity. The appeal is, at bottom, simply *It's true*. The following, from Charlotte Brontë's *Villette*, is a defense of this kind:

> I shall never forget that first lesson, nor all the undercurrent of life and character it opened up to me. Then first did I begin

rightly to see the wide difference that lies between the novelist's and poet's ideal "jeune fille" and the said "jeune fille" as she really is.[17]

If *Villette* is the feminist classic I take it to be, that is not because of any explicit feminist declarations made by the book but because of the novel's constant, passionate insistence that things are *like this* and not *like that*, from the pictures in the picture-gallery to Ginevra Fanshawe to John Bretton to Paulina-the-heroine (who at one point is actually compared to the school spaniel). Moers quotes another statement of Brontë's, more general, to the same effect:

> If men could see us as we really are, they would be a little amazed; but the cleverest, the acutest men are often under an illusion about women: they do not read them in a true light: they misapprehend them.[18]

Margaret Cavendish (who makes every sort of appeal) in a preface addressed to "the Two Most Famous Universities of England," after describing how men keep women ignorant and despise "the best of our Actions," appeals to:

> Learned Universities, where Nature is best known, where Truth is ofnest Found.... if I deserve not Praise ... Bury me in silence.... and who knows, but, after my Honorable Burial, I may have a Glorious Resurrection in Following Ages.[19]

Besides the appeal to truth (of which the Duchess is alternately optimistic and pessimistic, above) there is the appeal to former great women, that is, to models. In the seventeenth century the Countess of Winchilsea has to look rather far back for hers:

Sure 'twas not ever thus, nor are we told
Fables of Women that excell'd of old . . .
A woman here leads fainting Israel on,
She fights, she wins, she tryumphs with a song,
Devout, Majestick, for the subject fitt,
And far above her arms, exalts her witt,
Then to the peaceful, shady Palm withdraws,
And rules the rescu'd Nation, with her Laws.[20]

Pollution of agency via unchastity made it, I think, difficult to appeal to unblemished models in the nineteenth century. (Citing models for defense is not, of course, the same thing as using them for guidance in one's own work.) The great Sand, for example, wore pants, smoked cigars, and had lovers. George Eliot, for all the morality of her novels, was living with a man to whom she was not married. Who could claim them as blameless examples of great female writers? Indeed, if "immorality" doesn't exist, it can always be invented. Alexandra Kollontai, a feminist and communist contemporary of Lenin, was slandered by being declared promiscuous and an advocate of promiscuity. Her biographer, Irving Fetscher, declares "many legends and slanders (existed) among her enemies and followers alike. . . . According to the most famous . . . (she) is supposed to have declared that sexual contacts were as simple . . . as drinking a glass of water."[21] The biography is selections from Kollontai's writings with an afterword by Fetscher; in titillating and equally slanderous fashion, the book is entitled *The Autobiography of a Sexually Emancipated Communist Woman.* Emma Goldman called one of her male comrades a prig and "as with all our comrades, you are a puritan at heart. . . . Hundreds of men marry women much younger than themselves . . . they are accepted by the world. Everybody . . . resents, in fact dislikes a woman who lives with a younger man" (Goldman's situation); "it is not the business or concern of friends to make her look and feel like a fool. . . ."[22] According to Yi-tsi Feuerwerker, Ting Ling, the famous Communist Chinese feminist and writer, was criticized politically in the anti-rightist campaign of 1957 by a "stream of puritanical outrage . . . directed against Ting Ling's personal life as much as against her works. . . . One of the most striking features of the campaign was the total obliteration of any dividing line between the author and her fictional creations. . . . selected women in her fiction became incriminating 'self-portraits'" which betrayed "preoccupation with sex" and a "selfish desire to 'manipulate men.'" The author was accused of glorifying prostitution as "a blatant defense of (her) own immorality. . . . the charges of her sexual immorality were eagerly believed. . . . She was finally expelled and deprived of her rights as a citizen and a writer." Feuerwerker adds, "The heavily moralistic exploitation of the chastity problem . . . was not a concern when the targets of criticism were male."[23] Apparently, for women, sexual misbehavior is the one charge that can be relied upon to stick, even in "advanced" circles. So when the point at issue is the assumed inferiority of women's writing, appeal to models becomes unworkable without some kind of simultaneous attack on masculine privilege and the double standard, either *You won't accept my models because you're biased,* or *Great male writers are not blameless either,* or *How can there be any models when women have been so restricted?*

This is Anne Finch's strategy when she couples with her biblical example the protest that women are badly educated and punished by scorn if they attempt to achieve. Indeed, a direct attack on the statement *Women can't write* immediately shifts the ground from strategies of evasion, redefinition, or flight to a characteristic female literary response, this early version of which comes from JANE ANGER: "it was ANGER that did write it."[24] This response is not identical with feminism, although I suspect feminism is never without it and its presence always signals a kind of proto-feminism: personal protest, if not public. For example, Sylvia Plath was not a feminist, but if anything has made her into a feminist cult heroine, it is her entire and vehement disregard for the advice Woolf gave women writers in *A Room of One's Own:*

> It is fatal for a woman to lay the least stress on any grievance; to plead even with justice any cause; in any way to speak consciously as a woman.[25]

But Woolf did not always take her own advice. There are the cancelled passages in "Professions for Women" about gun-running, window-smashing, and armored tanks, as well as the ones she left in (but Leonard Woolf didn't): the imagination "in a state of fury ... panting with rage and disappointment" at being checked by the reason because it will be "fifty years" before a woman can speak the truth about her body. Although Woolf adds in this speech that women must not add "the burden of bitterness" to their other burdens,[26] there is bitterness aplenty in *Three Guineas.* Woolf recorded feelings of "immense relief and peace" at the completion of the book, adding "Now I am quit of that *poison and excitement*"[27] (italics mine). In "Art and Anger" Marcus notes, "The one characteristic of her 'madness' was the expression of extreme anger and hostility."[28] There are other examples: Mary Ellmann's passionate irony in a cause she finally declares best not fought at all and Margaret Cavendish flashing out, "Women live like Bats or Owls, labour like Beasts, and die like Worms...."[29] Woolf calls the Duchess verbose and rage something that "disfigured and deformed" her, but she's certainly not verbose here; anger spurs her to eloquence. Indeed Moers finds anger one of the hallmarks of women's writing and gives it as the reason "why chattel slavery was a woman's literary subject in the epic age." Earlier she stated, of *Jane Eyre:*

Brontë makes her speaker both a person and a female in the quickest shorthand available to women writers: she has her say no.[30]

It is difficult sometimes to know how anger may be avoided. Joan Goulianos, in the introduction to *By a Woman Writt*, quotes "an eminent [male] scholar" confronted with *The Book of Margery Kempe*:

Poor Margery is to be classed with those hotels which Baedeker describes as "variously judged." You must come to her not expecting too much, and prepared for anything.[31]

Why does a scholar call a woman a hotel? Does he expect to sleep in her? And does "anything" indicate his dislike of female content, or is it necessary to explain what he already knows, that Margery Kempe was illiterate and often poor, and had dictated this document (with great trouble) to various people who could write, over a period of years?

And yet there is beginning to be a response that goes beyond anger. Nowadays the statement *Women can't write* sometimes meets with neither strategies for evasion and redefinition, nor the appeal to truth, nor the appeal to models, nor even a direct confrontation, but a drastic shift in perspective which can only occur in the context of explicit feminism, after considerable open anger, and with the backing of feminist solidarity. This is a response I can only call *woman-centeredness*. Thus, when Hacker writes, "It was very exciting to see them, a past, *our* past,"[32] or Judy Chicago responds to self-portraits of Rosalba Carriera and Judith Leyster by being "deeply moved. I felt I was seeing an echo of my identity as an artist across the centuries,"[33] neither woman is appealing to a model in order to prove to anyone that *Women can't create* is false. Their concern is with kinship, that is, with each other. The author of *Literary Women* can speak without apology of "the great feminist decade of the 1790s, when Mary Wollstonecraft blazed and died" and delight in "a golden harvest of memoirs by distinguished women . . . [of] the past decade." Moers adds that her book is "plainly a celebration of the great women who have spoken for us all, whatever our sex,"[34] a magnificently placid appropriation of the cliché of "universality" for women writers. This sort of thing is easier to do in criticism than in art, but I would place next to *Literary Women* a novel like Bertha Harris' *Lover*[35] in which there is a mythic reordering of the entire cosmos around women, including genealogical tables. The prerequisite for both works is feminist solidarity. Woolf glimpsed this possibility, I think, in the talks given to all-female audiences at Newnham and Girton (the papers that were the origin of *A Room of One's Own*), though she could not sustain it. Indeed, in order to present her audience with such a startling revelation, she had first to assure herself that they *were* all women. Woolf has been discussing her fictitious novelist, Mary Carmichael, and Carmichael's novel, significantly entitled *Life's Adventure*. But she breaks off:

> . . . I am sorry to break off abruptly. Are there no men present? . . . We are all women, you assure me? Then I may tell you that the very next words I read were these—"Chloe liked Olivia. . . ." Do not start. Do not blush. Let us admit in the privacy of our own society that these things sometimes happen. Sometimes women do like women.
>   "Chloe liked Olivia," I read. And then it struck me how immense a change was there.[36]

Woolf goes on to explain that the change is a change in literature. But it is also a change in life. No longer must a feminist as brilliant as Woolf ask—even comically—whether men are present before she feels free to ally herself with other women. The practical difficulties remain immense, but there are now women's presses which not only assume a female audience, but the central importance, both aesthetic and political, of such an audience. There are feminist journals which do the same. Here is Moers remaking the universe:

> The poet is representative. She stands among partial women for the complete woman. . . . The young woman reveres women of genius because, to speak truly, they are more herself than she is. . . . For all women live by truth and stand in need of expression.
>
> EMERSON[37]

More and more the claim *Women can't write* is being answered not by redefinitions or by evasions, or by appeals to models, or to truth, or even by direct confrontation and anger (except as a deliberate, public tactic). This newest response is even more disturbing:

It's a *What?* from a group of turned-away, preoccupied female backs.

11.
Aesthetics

T HE REEVALUATION AND rediscovery of minority art (including the cultural minority of women) is often conceived as a matter of remedying injustice and exclusiveness through doing justice to individual artists by allowing their work into the canon, which will thereby be more complete, but fundamentally unchanged. Sometimes it's also stressed that the erasing of previous injustice will encourage new artists of the hitherto "wrong" groups and thus provide art with more artists who will provide new (or different) material—and that all of this activity will enrich, but not change, the canon of art itself.

But in the case of women, what has been left out? "Merely," says Carolyn Kizer, "the private lives of one-half of humanity."[1]

These lives are not lived in isolation from the private and public lives of the other half. Here is Jean Baker Miller describing what happens when the lives of half a community are omitted from the consciousness of the other half:

Some of the areas of life denied by the dominant group are ... projected on to all subordinate groups. ... But other parts of experience are so necessary that they cannot be projected very far away. One must *have* them nearby, even if one can still deny *owning* them. These are the special areas delegated to women.

She adds:

... when ... women move out of their restricted place, they threaten men in a very profound sense with the need to reintegrate many of the essentials of human development. ... These things have been warded off and become doubly fearful because they look as if they will entrap men in "emotions," weakness, sexuality, vulnerability, helplessness, the need for care, and other unsolved areas.

And:

Inevitably the dominant group is the model for "normal human relationships." It then becomes normal to treat others destructively and to derogate them, to obscure the truth of what you are doing by creating false explanations ... to keep on doing these things, one need only behave "normally."[2]

A mode of understanding life that wilfully ignores so much can do so only at the peril of thoroughly distorting the rest. A mode of understanding literature that can ignore the private lives of half the human race is not "incomplete"; it is distorted through and through. Feminist criticism of the early 1970s began by pointing out the simplest of these distortions, that is, that the female characters of even our greatest realistic "classics" by male writers are often not individualized portraits of possible women, but creations of fear and desire. At best, according to Lillian Robinson:

> ... the problem is ... [whether] the author, in showing what goes on in a heroine's mind, is showing us anything like the mind of an actual human female. .... I am amazed at how many writers have chosen to evade it by externalizing the psychological situation, using "objective" images that convey the pattern or content of a woman's thought without actually entering into it. ... Emma Bovary and Anna Karenina, to name two eminently successful literary creations, are realized for us in this way.[3]

Some literary creations are not so successful or so innocuous, from Dickens' incapacity to portray women alone or in solely female society to Hemingway's misogynistic daydreams. I am thinking especially of Dickens' Bella Wilfer in *Our Mutual Friend*, vain and pretty, who flirts (quite reasonably) with her father, then applies the same manner to her younger sister (which is not reasonable) and then—alone—flirts (impossibly) with her mirror. Women speaking of mirrors and prettiness make it all too clear that even for pretty women, mirrors are the foci of anxious, not gratified, narcissism. The woman who knows beyond a doubt that she is beautiful exists aplenty in male novelists' imaginations; I have yet to find her in women's books or women's memoirs or in life. Women spend a lot of time looking in mirrors, but the "compulsion to visualize the self" is a phrase Moers uses of women in her chapter on Gothic freaks and horrors; the compulsion is a constant check on one's (possible) beauty, not an enjoyment of it. Dickens' error is simple; how could he have observed the Bellas of his world alone or heard their thoughts? So he simply extends public behavior into a private situation. Here is Annis Pratt, on that incarnation of the eternal feminine, Molly Bloom:

> It is difficult not to feel about Molly Bloom on her chamber-pot what Eldridge Cleaver must feel about Jack Benny's Rochester, but a good critic will not withdraw her attention from a work which is resonant and craftsmanlike even if it is chauvinistic.[4]

Robinson, answering Pratt in the same issue of the same journal, refuses to take so mild a position:

> sexual stereotypes serve *somebody's* interest.... I believe only a feminist knows what Molly Bloom is really about and can ask the questions that will demonstrate the real functioning of sexual myth in Joyce's novel.[5]

In the same issue, Dolores Barracano Schmidt performs this investigation in an essay on "The Great American Bitch," calling this twentieth-century character who appears in men's novels

> more myth than reality, a fabrication used to maintain the *status quo*. She is a figure about whom a whole cluster of values and taboos clings: women's fight for equality was a mistake ... women are not equipped for civilization.... by being so thoroughly hateful the Great American Bitch of fiction reinforces the sexist view.[6]

Another feminist critic, Cynthia Griffin Wolff, generalizes:

> The definition [in literature] of women's most serious problems and the proposed solutions ... are ... covertly tailored to meet the needs of fundamentally *masculine* problems....

women appear in literature . . . as conveniences to the resolution of masculine dilemmas.

One of Wolff's examples is the opposition of "virtuous" to "sensuous" woman, a projection of a male split in feeling and value which "relieves . . . [the man] from the difficulties of trying to unite two forces of love." (The "sensuous" woman, as Wolff points out, is not one who desires men but one who is desired by them.) She goes on:

> men may appear stereotypically . . . but the stereotype [e.g., the Warrior] is usually a fantasied solution to an essentially masculine problem. . . . Moreover, there is a . . . significant body of literature which recognizes the limitations of some of these masculine stereotypes [e.g., *The Red Badge of Courage*]. There is no comparable body of anti-stereotype literature about women. . . . Even women writers . . . seem to adopt them.[7]

Judith Fetterley offers even more telling examples:

> . . . when I look at a poem like "The Solitary Reaper" . . . I do not find my experience in it at all. Rather I find that the drama of the poem depends upon a contrast between the male subject as conscious, creative knower and the unknowing female object of his contemplation; it is my wordless, artless, natural and utterly unself-conscious song which has provided the male speaker/poet with the opportunity to define himself as knower. . . . [in "To His Coy Mistress"] the complexity of the speaker's situation, which is the subject of the poem, is modest compared to the complexity of the mistress's position . . . [which is] the essence of *my* relation to the poem.

Elsewhere she states one of the central problems of feminist criticism:

> What happens to one's definition of aesthetic criteria . . . when one is confronted by a literature which does not support the self but assaults it[?][8]

Vonda McIntyre answers:

> Right now a lot of literary and film "classics" are unbearable . . . because of the underlying [sexist] assumptions. In a few generations I think they will be either incomprehensible or so ridiculous as to be funny.[9]

And Ellen Cantarow, looking into her college textbook, finds that next to Pope's line, "Most women have no Characters at all," she once wrote: "SPEAKER. TONE. DEFINE." She asks:

> Where in my notes was that other girl, the girl who once raged at being taken for "a typical Wellesley *girl*?" . . . [there was] intense self-hatred . . . education at Wellesley . . . didn't just belie our life experience as girls . . . it nullified that experience, rendered it invisible. . . . we lived in a state of schizophrenia that we took to be normal.[10]

A more explicit, systematic rejection of the canon and the standards that support it can be found in the field of art—a rejection I believe parallel to that going on in a more piecemeal fashion in literature. For example, Mary Garrard asks:

> Why is our art history . . . full of virtuous reversals in which a virile, heroic, or austere style suddenly and dramatically replaces a feminine, lyrical, or luxurious one—David

over Fragonard, Caravaggio over Salviati, clean international Modern Gropius over wickedly ornamental Sullivan or Tiffany?[11]

Valerie Jaudon and Joyce Kozloff answer:

The prejudice against the decorative has a long art history and is based on hierarchies: fine art above decorative art, Western art above non-Western art, men's art above women's art ... "high art" [means] man, mankind, the individual man, individuality, humans, humanity, the human figure, humanism, civilization, culture, the Greeks, the Romans, the English, Christianity, spiritual transcendence, religion, nature, true form, science, logic, creativity, action, war, virility, violence, brutality, dynamism, power, and greatness.

In the same texts other words are used repeatedly in connection with ... "low art": Africans, Orientals, Persians, Slovaks, peasants, the lower classes, women, children, savages, pagans, sensuality, pleasure, decadence, chaos, anarchy, impotence, exotica, eroticism, artifice, tattoos, cosmetics, ornaments, decoration, carpets, weaving, patterns, domesticity, wallpaper, fabrics, and furniture.

The rest of Jaudon and Kozloff's essay consists of quotations from artists and art historians arranged under such headings as "War and Virility," "Purity in Art as a Holy Cause," and a particularly damning section expressing "the desire for unlimited personal power," which the authors call "Autocracy."[12]

Such associations of art with virility, quality with size, and authenticity with self-aggrandizement appear in literature, too. (One of the strangest conversations I ever had was with a male colleague who stated that Chekhov could not be a "great" artist because he never wrote anything "full-length." In some confusion—apparently short stories and novellas didn't count—I mentioned the plays. These, it seemed, didn't count either; "they're much shorter than novels," said my colleague.) Here is Adrienne Rich, pointing out that the "masterpieces" we have been taught to admire are not merely flawed, but that they may not even mean what we have been taught they mean. In "The Ninth Symphony of Beethoven Understood at Last as a Sexual Message," Rich begins with "A man in terror of impotence," and goes on to describe the music as

> music of the entirely
> isolated soul
> yelling at Joy from the tunnel of the ego
> music without the ghost
> of another person in it. . . .

What is the man trying to say? Something he would keep back if he could, "bound and flogged" with "chords of Joy." The real situation behind all this pounding?

> . . . everything is silence and the
> beating of a bloody fist upon
> a splintered table.[13]

If the canon is an attempt to shore up the status quo, if the masterpieces don't mean what they pretend to mean, then artists must throw away the rules altogether in favor of something else. "Their musty rules of unity, and God knows what besides, if they meant anything," says Aphra Behn, but she goes no further.[14] Rich does, stating:

> in pretending to stand for "the human," masculine subjectivity tries to force us to name our truths in an alien language,

to dilute them; we are constantly told that the "real" problems . . . are those men have defined, that the problems we need to examine are trivial, unscholarly, nonexistent . . .
Any woman who has moved from the playing-fields of male discourse into the realm where women are developing our own descriptions of the world, knows the extraordinary sense of shedding . . . someone else's baggage, of ceasing to translate. It is not that thinking becomes easy, but that the difficulties are intrinsic to the work itself, rather than to the environment . . .[15]

In "ceasing to translate," the "wrong" people begin to make not only good, but genuinely experimental, art. Several contemporary women's theatre groups have thrown away not only the unities but the lights, the proscenium, the elaborate impressiveness, the "primitivism," and the assault-on-the-audience that marked the theatrical "experiments" of the 1960s. Contemporaneously with the reappearance of feminism, these women's groups have instead created a version of Epic Theatre (though nobody's noticed): much narrative, constantly changing characters, many incidents (personal and historical), direct (and sympathetic) commentary to the audience, and the reenactment, sometimes in mime, rather than the here-and-now "hot" acting, of important scenes. These performances are, to my mind, more genuinely experimental than what passed for experimental theatre in the 1960s, just as Baldwin's nonfiction is not only beautiful but genuinely experimental in comparison (for example) with much Joyce- or Nabokov-derived modern work. We have been trained to regard certain kinds of art (especially the violent, the arcane, and the assaultive) as "experimental." But there's all the difference in the world between studying oxidation and producing loud noises with gunpowder. The former leads somewhere; the latter (analogous to rock groups' raising the ante with decibelage, luridness, and violence) does not.

There are genuine experiments happening in women's writing. According to Suzanne Juhasz, "In the late sixties and early seventies an explosion of poetry by women occurred. . . ." She goes on, concluding that women are being forced to create new poetic forms, since:

> If the woman poet wants . . . to link her particular experiences with larger universals . . . she can call upon only a percentage of her own experiences. Much of what she knows does not link up to universals because the universals presently in existence are based upon masculine experience, masculine norms.

One way of dealing with the norms of what is or is not universal is to ignore them and relate particulars to particulars. This leads to writing (as Juhasz puts it) in the vernacular and not in Latin. It also leads to rejection slips, as she finds out:

> Recently I received a rejection slip from a well-meaning editor who, while admitting the "necessary" nature of my poems, took issue with the fact that my poems "said it all." "Try more denotation, synecdoche, metonymy, suggestion," he said. Yet I and many feminist poets do not want to treat poetry as a metalanguage that needs to be decoded.[16]

Julia Penelope, also, notes the critics' annoyance when "works . . . make the function of the critic obsolete. The . . . work . . . (is) immediately available to the reader, and there is no need for the . . . intervention of the critic as guide or explicator."[17] Noting that the epigram is, by tradition, inferior to the epic, Juhasz quotes with delight some of Alta's short poems, for example:

> if you won't make love to me, at least
> get out of my dreams!

Here's another, by black poet Pat Parker, to white women:

> SISTER! your foot's smaller
> but it's still on my neck.

Juhasz finally abandons the idea of the canon altogether:

> A poem works if it lives up to itself. Such a definition contains no built-in ranking system.[18]

And here is Woolf's opinion of the canon:

> They [the children] knew what he liked best—to be forever walking up and down, up and down, with Mr. Ramsay, and saying who had won this, who had won that, who was a "first-rate man" . . . who was "brilliant but . . . fundamentally unsound," who was "undoubtedly the ablest fellow in Bailliol." . . . That was what they talked about.[19]

But if we throw out the linear hierarchy, are we to do without standards altogether? Here is Juhasz again:

> Yet a poem can work and not be good. It can be dull or ordinary or superficial. A *good* poem works *powerfully* and *accurately* to communicate between poet and reader or listener.[20] [italics mine]

But which reader? Which listener? The techniques for mystifying women's lives and belittling women's writing that I have described work by suppressing context: writing is separated from experience, women writers are separated from their tradition and each other, public is separated from private, political from personal—all to enforce a supposed set of absolute standards. What is frightening about black art or women's art or Chicano art—and so on—is that it calls into question the very idea of objectivity and absolute standards:

This is a good novel.

Good *for what?*

Good *for whom?*

One side of the nightmare is that the privileged group will not recognize that "other" art, will not be able to judge it, that the superiority of taste and training possessed by the privileged critic and the privileged artist will suddenly vanish.

The other side of the nightmare is not that what is found in the "other" art will be incomprehensible, but that it will be all too familiar. That is:

Women's lives are the buried truth about men's lives.

The lives of people of color are the buried truth about white lives.

The buried truth about the rich is who they take their money from and how.

The buried truth about "normal" sexuality is how one kind of sexual expression has been made privileged, and what kinds of unearned virtue and terrors about identity this distinction serves.

There are other questions: why is "greatness" in art so often aggressive? Why does "great" literature have to be long? Is "regionalism" only another instance of downgrading the vernacular? Why is "great" architecture supposed to knock your eye out at first view, unlike "indigenous" architecture, which must be appreciated slowly and with knowledge of the climate in which it exists? Why is the design of clothing—those grotesque and sometimes perilously fantastic anatomical-social-role-characterological ideas of the person—a "minor" art? Because it has a use? In admiring "pure" (i.e., useless) art, are we not merely admiring Veblenian conspicuous consumption, like the Mandarin fingernail? In Eve Merriam's recent play "The Club" it became clear that masculine and feminine body language are very different; gestures socially recognizable as "male" lay claim to as much space as possible, while comparable "female" gestures are self-protective, self-referential, and take up as little space as possible.

Male reviewers, astonished at a play in which the members of a nineteenth-century men's club *and* the club's black waiter *and* its boy in buttons *and* its piano player were all played by women, praised the actresses for their success in imitating men without making any attempt to hide their own female anatomy. In her autobiography Judy Chicago comments:

> When the women "acted out" walking down the street and being accosted by men, everyone seemed able to "take on" the characteristics of the tough swagger, of men "coming on." It was as if they knew the words so well.[21]

Male reviewers understood the point of hearing sexist jokes and songs of the period performed by women, but it took a female reviewer (in *Harper's Bazaar*, I think) to see that the final effect of seeing women in the habiliments of power was utter confusion as to what roles belonged to whom. She called this disappearance of the link between gender and sexual physiology the labels washing off the bottles; I came out of the theater saying, "But what *is* 'women'?" Perhaps this isn't the effect the play had on men, or perhaps male reviewers were not being honest. I think it would be unlikely if a play like this had an identical effect on women and on men.

In art, are we (in fact) trained to admire body language? An obviously aggressive or forceful technique? Loudness? These questions are being asked and dealt with. But they cannot be (and are not being) dealt with by assuming one absolute center of value.

In everybody's present historical situation, there can be, I believe, no single center of value and hence no absolute standards. That does not mean that assignment of values must be arbitrary or self-serving (like my students, whose defense of their poetry is "I felt it"). It does mean that for the linear hierarchy of good and bad it becomes necessary to substitute a multitude of centers of value, each with its own periphery, some closer to each other, some farther apart. The centers have been constructed by the historical facts of what it is to be female or black or working class or what-have-you; when we all live in the same culture, then it will be time for one literature. But that is not the case now. Nor is there one proper "style." There are many kinds of English (including Anglo-Indian) and before determining whether (for example) Virginia Woolf "writes better than" Zora Neale Hurston, it might be a good idea to decide who is addressing the mind's ear and who the mind's eye—in short, *what* English we're talking about. One is a kind of Latin, sculptured, solid, and distinct, into which comes the vernacular from time to time; the other is literary-as-vernacular: fluid, tone-shifting, visually fleeting, with the (impossible) cadences of the mind's ear constantly overriding the memory of the physical ear. (Woolf often writes sentences too long for any but the most experienced actor to speak as a single breath-unit.) If the one kind of English is too slow and too eternally set, is not the other kind too facile, too quick, always a little too thin?

There used to be an odd, popular, and erroneous idea that the sun revolved around the earth.

This has been replaced by an even odder, equally popular, and equally erroneous idea that the earth goes around the sun.

In fact, the moon and the earth revolve around a common center, and this commonly-centered pair revolves with the sun around another common center, except that you must figure in all the solar planets here, so things get complicated. Then there is the motion of the solar system with regard to a great many other objects, e.g., the galaxy, and if at this point you ask *what does the motion of the earth really look like from the center of the entire universe*, say (and where are the Glotolog?), the only answer is: that it doesn't.

Because there isn't.

Epilogue

A conviction has been growing on me throughout the writing of this oddly sized and oddly shaped piece.

There is much, much more good literature by women in existence than anyone knows.

There is more of it than I had any idea of when I began writing this. Again and again women burst into the official canon as if from nowhere—eccentric, peculiar, with techniques that look odd and preoccupations that don't "fit." Sometimes they get into the canon because they can be described in sexist terms. (Carolyn Kizer, in "Pro Femina," chides Elizabeth Barrett Browning for saddling female writers with the myth of the devoted wife, but although EBB's life may lend itself to that myth, she certainly didn't create it—it was there before she arrived—and she certainly didn't promulgate it after her death.) Jane Austen read widely in women's novels and was even afraid to read Mary Brunton's *Self-Control* while revising *Sense and Sensibility* because she was afraid of finding it "too clever" and her own story and characters "all forestalled."[1] Yet (as Moers points out), who reads Mary Brunton's novels now, or can even find them? Brunton has been relegated to the dustbin of history along with Mrs. Georgie Sheldon and Ouida, whom I know to be bad novelists because I've read them. But I never even heard of Mary Brunton's *Self-Control* before reading *Literary Women*.

But is not the judgment of one of the greatest novelists in English to be trusted somewhat above that of male scholars reading art that comes from experiences they have not had and do not believe important? Or, if not trusted, at least investigated? Was Mary Brunton that bad a novelist? Was Anna Maria Porter that bad? Was the compressed, direct-address style of the eighteenth-century female romance merely a bad style or was it—as Palomo suggests—a style modeled on the French romance, one developed to express concerns completely foreign to (say) the author of *Tom Jones*?[2] Women's social concerns haven't changed that much in nearly two centuries; I once made a women's studies class (in the middle of Book Two of *Emma*) gasp simply by asking:

"Who gave the piano to Jane Fairfax?"

(Those who were in the know looked gleefully smug; one young woman clasped her hands over an incipient shriek; and another turned pale and said, "Oh my God." This is what happens when you no longer have to translate what you read.)

What about the influences on Emily Dickinson?

For that matter, working-class authors (like Melville) enter the canon similarly shorn of their cultural context. I have read several pieces of criticism about "Bartleby" and although one of them compared Melville's position to Carlyle's Eternal No, not one of them began, "Did you ever work on an assembly line for ten years?" (Or in Woolworth's for six months or typing address labels for as little as one summer?) These questions are very much to the point, as I and H. Bruce Franklin see the story.[3] But then I worked as a secretary for three years and typed address labels for a mere six weeks—and that six weeks was enough to reveal Bartleby's situation to me as twenty years of reading literary criticism could not. (In a recent collection of Melville's stories, Harold Beaver sums up his remarks on "Bartleby" as follows: "Bartleby can never be wholly interpreted as either . . . Christ-figure, artist, or ascetic saint, nor is the story exhausted by such interpretations. At its root lies a theme more compelling than both: of the *doppleganger*... the figure of death... behind the green screen" of life.[4] The actual nature of Bartleby's work—its isolation, its rote nature, its hideous boredom—and the social situation of employer-employee, as well as Bartleby's sitdown strike and the sentimental liberalism of his employer, are never mentioned.)

The amount of experience left out of the official literary canon is simply staggering. Yet sometimes writers are let in by a fluke of association with a "school" (but did James Joyce invent stream-of-consciousness, or did Dorothy Richardson?) or sheer verbal gift (like Emily Dickinson) (and the patriotic desire to find a good nineteenth-century American writer—remember the cultural inferiority complex of the 1920s and 1930s). There is no effort, however, to find out the origins of these strange people; like comets they flash across the horizon, coming from outer darkness and leaving no influence behind them.

Whom did the Brontës influence?

Well, me. I read *Jane Eyre* at twelve and ritually reread it every year thereafter until I hit sixteen and a college education that included it (but not *Villette* or *Shirley* or Emily Brontë's Gondal poems). I read *Wuthering Heights*, starting at fourteen and returning frequently until my late teens. In college I read Woolf's novels secretly and guiltily, like bonbons; I was ashamed of them because they were so "feminine."

Yet I never dreamed of thinking of these women's books as "literary influences," and when I dedicated my second novel, it was to what I then thought of as real literary influences, both male: S. J. Perelman (daringly) and Vladimir Nabokov.

From what tradition did the Brontës come? Only the moors and Byron, it seemed, until Moers "discovered" that Charlotte, at least, seemed to know and correspond with a number of people, many of them women, some of them even writers.

In a lecture on women's painting given at the University of Colorado in the spring of 1977, J. J. Wilson made one crucial point: *Nobody ever paints just one picture.* (Although, she added, if you knew women artists only by popular reproductions, you might think so.)

It is the same in literature. No one—except one who dies at sixteen—writes one novel and nothing else. No one produces one small group of poems and nothing else. Nobody is without origins. Nobody is totally without colleagues. Nobody whose work is read at all is without influence.

There are telltale signs of premature burial all over the official canon; I suggest that just as Wilson and Petersen's investigations of male artists revealed great numbers of female ones who had been recategorized as wives, mothers, daughters, and mistresses, careful investigation of the lives of female authors we do know will undoubtedly reveal a great number we don't. Their art will not look like what we're used to, but a tradition that can treat "Bartleby" as if Melville were a sort of Carlyle-philosophizing-in-his-study is capable of anything, even of presenting certain very limited standards as universal.

I suspect that women's writing (I mean by this middle-class white women's writing, as will be clear presently) has tended to take certain shapes and use certain techniques we aren't used to. For one thing, it has tended to be visionary, like Dickinson's poems, like those sudden magnificent breaks in Charlotte Brontë's books, in which inward vision suddenly erupts through the surface of ordinary life (Lucy's madness during the long vacation is such a break in *Villette*, as is Jane's vision of the female moon in *Jane Eyre*). Like Blake, for that matter, or Melville, or the passionate preaching with which Agnes Smedley's *Daughter of Earth* is flawed—and starred. After all, working-class people don't know a damn about "good taste" and the unity of tone and style (nobody ever taught them, the poor sods) and when they do find out, they're apt to be exasperated at the unnecessariness of such niceties—rather like Aphra Behn, in *her* blunt, uneducated way (so sad), growling about the musty unities and "God knows what." And middle-class women, although taught to value established forms, are in the same position as the working class: neither can use established forms to express what the forms were never intended to express (and may very well operate to conceal). In addition, women *qua* women have the terrible burden of the "narrowness" of their experience. Hence the lack of unity, the rocking and cracking of the book as the inadequate form strains or even collapses, or the hideously difficult attempt to keep the white heat of the visionary going through a whole book—Virginia Woolf and Herman Melville are sister and brother here, Woolf convinced of her lack of experience (she refers very often in her nonfiction to women's narrowness of experience and her own lack of a university education), Melville with the wrong kind of experience.

Has nobody ever noticed the extreme unevenness of style and tone in *Moby Dick?* It is full of discontinuities, jerks, sudden wrenches, gear-changes, a real defect, although probably the only way the book could have been written at all. And reading *Pierre* is like trying to ride a bronco. Both books are, I think, blood kin to Woolf's welding everything into one huge knot of intense subjectivity. Both writers are coping with what is *unspeakable* in the accepted forms. Joyce, who perfected certain forms and then enriched them and opened them up to the point where they turn into something new, is not, I think, engaged in the same process at all. He is coping with the desire to say *more* than the current realism can say, but he is not trying to express *other* than it can say. His changes of style in, say, *Ulysses*, are intensely literary and under control; Melville's do not seem so to me, although modern scholars—once they made him into that sacred figure, a great writer—have, I think, turned cartwheels to bestow on him a unity of style and tone which he does not have. (Chapters 27 ["Sunset"], and 29 ["First Night Watch"] and 40 ["Midnight Forecastle"] suddenly break into theatrical soliloquy and dialogue. This purple patch is the worst break in the whole work, to my mind.) D. H. Lawrence, another child of the working class, seems to me to belong in the same company; his writing is certainly as polemical, as spasmodic, as broken, as— say—*Daughter of Earth*.

What happens to women who accept the forms? One possibility is deceit, evasion, slyness. A mind in a sense too big for its material, which is (we are constantly reminded) only a romance, only a novel, only the very private, very limited lives of people who are, after all, not terribly important. And don't worry; you will meet only propriety, only the smallest, most domestic events, only the Iron Hand in the Velvet Glove, so well done (in one case) that for quite a while many saw only the glove— "gentle Jane," whom Vladimir Nabokov, lecturing at Cornell University in 1956, called "a kitten." Modern criticism does much more justice to the Iron Hand, but without investigating whether a similar one might not be under the surface of (say) *Self-Control*—or Dorothy Sayers' detective stories. I begin to suspect something complex and very interesting—a kind of tragedy—might emerge from the Peter Wimsey books, read as one big book. Kathi Maio traces the changes in the central character in *Whose Body* (1923) through *Busman's Honeymoon* (1937) and the social implications of these changes, but doesn't suggest that the works be read as one work.[5] I would call the vision that emerges not only the (obvious) Christian ideal of how life should be lived—not aristocracy, which is qualified somewhat but not nearly enough as the series proceeds (these are very snobbish books)—but an increasing knowledge of how chancy and how threatened such happiness is. It finally breaks down altogether in *Busman's Honeymoon*, which ends, as Maio notes, with Wimsey having what amounts to a nervous breakdown in despair at the impossibility of combining justice with mercy in the real world.

Another alternative is sheer fantasy, like the melodramas the author of *Little Women* wrote and later regretted, like ... well, like Ouida (I had better reread her), like those Gothic romances routinely ignored—but again, Mrs. Radcliffe was not a single, anomalous birth, like Athena from the head of Jove, and I doubt that all her colleagues were uniformly beneath contempt. After all, without the proper experiences of life, without a form you can use, unable to say anything realistic or straightforward, why not speak dream language? Especially if you can pretend it's realism. So Brockden Brown is admired as a fantasist while the author of *Charlotte Temple* is a nitwit—maybe. But *Charlotte Temple* is surely as much fantasy as *Alice in Wonderland*.

And very little attention has been paid to the romances written by women through the eighteenth century, or to Rebecca Harding Davis's rough, fantastic stories of women who were artists and were so terribly punished for it. Those didn't come from nowhere, either. It is now known that Kafka (once considered just such an anomalous artist) had behind him a whole tradition of Yiddish fantasists (they went serenely on into the early twentieth century). Once it's admitted that art need not be "unified," "comprehensive," and "big" in order to be "great" (some confusion here between "big" and "great," no?), what treasures may we not find! Again, when Byron does it, he's at least all right (modern criticism is, in fact, nervous about Byron's romantic work and prefers him as a satirist), but when Louisa May Alcott does it, nobody even knows it exists.

(When I became aware [in college] of my "wrong" experience, I chose fantasy. Convinced that I had no real experience of

life, since my own obviously wasn't part of Great Literature, I
decided consciously that I'd write of things nobody knew anything about, dammit. So I wrote realism disguised as fantasy,
that is, science fiction.)

To read the visionary's blazes of illumination as faulty structure, fantasy as if it were failed realism, to read subversion as if
it were nothing but its surface, is automatically to condemn
minority writing, among which is the writing of women. When
critics have to deal with a different English, there is also the ploy
of reading the difference as if it were failure. With Anglo-Indian
or Anglo-African (like Chinua Achebe) such judgments are usually avoided, but when the writers live in the United States and
are *supposed* to be speaking English . . . well, we all know what
English is and it's not like that.

There is a false center to "literature." It's not only male, white,
and middle class (or above) but also European East Coast. Whatever happened to that splendid burst of conscious American-
ness which produced people like Willa Cather, Sherwood Anderson, Carl Sandburg, Sinclair Lewis, and (somewhat later) Thomas
Wolfe? Criticism seems to find them embarrassing nowadays
and prefers the expatriate Hemingway, the expatriate Eliot, and
the expatriate Pound. It seems that "universal" does not include
"American." And yet I encountered a passage from *Main Street*
the other day that set my hair on end with pleasure. And up in
Canada Alice Munro and Margaret Lawrence are being region-
alists all over again. The poor dears seem not to care how very
non-universal they are.

Perhaps the following may explain why.

No sooner had I finished writing the body of this essay than
a (female) colleague at the University of Colorado called me.
I mentioned this project to her and casually added that I was
assuming no women had written in English prior to about 1600.

"Better not do that," she said.

"What?" said I. (Alps upon Alps arise.)

"Sure," she said. "You know, to be really educated you had to learn Latin—it was an upper-class male puberty rite—but there were women who learned Latin. We don't know of many, but there were some. Mostly they translated religious works into the vernacular, or wrote devotional works themselves, in the vernacular. Like Henry VIII's last wife, remember? You saw her on television; you should know."

"Oops," said I. (Well, such is the power of rubricizing; it wasn't *my* fault, I just—)

My friend said, "Women always write in the vernacular."

Women always write in the vernacular.

Not strictly true, and yet it explains a lot. It certainly explains letters and diaries. And Nin's choice of the diary as the quintessentially feminine form. It explains why so many women wrote ghost stories in the nineteenth century and still write them; in fact, one of the most interesting stories of the supernatural I ever read was by a woman active in the 1930s, Margaret Irwin,[6] though Bleiler's introduction to a collection of the works of the nineteenth-century novelist Sheridan LeFanu smugly places him as superior to his three (female) contemporaries.[7] And Margaret Irwin's collected works are not, it seems, in print anywhere today, though LeFanu's are. This is not to deny LeFanu's achievement. Yet I suspect that LeFanu's father-son conflict, his theme of the "disinherited hero," would interest critics more than Irwin's portrayal of the corruption of masculine values. As Woolf once said of the difference between male and female interests, naturally this is so. And here is another fascinating instance of the vernacular, from Alma Murch:

> When the outcry against "sensation novels" was at its height in the 1850s and 1860s, the contemporary critics were considerably disturbed because so many of them were written by

women. . . . publishers seemed to feel there was something peculiarly indelicate about tales of crime or criminals being written by a woman, and were reluctant to print them.[8]

(Is M. R. James a woman? Apparently not. But P. D. James is. E. X. Ferrars is. So are Tobias Wells, Anthony Gilbert, and James Tiptree Jr. Had I but known what fascinating secret lurked behind yon initials—or yon pseudonyms—culture might have been a little less disheartening, a little less mystifying.)

In the vernacular it's also hard to be "classic," to be smooth, to be perfect. The Sacred Canon of Literature quite often pretends that some works can be not only atemporal and universal (that is, outside of history, a religious claim) but without flaw and without perceptible limitations. It's hard, in the vernacular, to pretend this, to paper over the cracks. It's also hard to read the vernacular as Holy Writ (which some critics still do, interpreting even the typographical errors as genius).

Minority art, vernacular art, is marginal art. Only on the margins does growth occur. Which is why, in the feminist movement, *Sexual Politics* was written by a sculptor, *Amazon Odyssey* by a philosopher of art (Ti-Grace Atkinson), and *Man's World, Woman's Place* by a novelist. And why I, who am a science-fiction writer and not a scholar, must wrestle in my not-very-abundant spare time with this ungainly monster. Because you, you critics, have not already done so (preferably a century ago).

If you don't like my book, write your own.

Please!

But remember, one can't get minority work into the canon by pretending it's about the same things or uses the same techniques as majority work. It probably isn't and doesn't. It may very well look like nothing ever before seen on earth. When science fiction first entered academia, the mistakes made about it by critics were grotesque. They continue to be, from time to time. This was due not only to a lack of scientific background—for example, some critics saw classic alien-background stories as nightmares, being unaware of the accuracy of the background and the delight in this as the story's point—but also to a lack of any knowledge of the field's history and conventions (including lack of the knowledge that it *had* a history and conventions).

But there is no political reason for critics to reject or misconceive or ignore science fiction. There's plenty of reason for them to do all three with women's writing. (An example is Nzotake Shange's play, *For Colored Girls Who Have Considered Suicide When the Rainbow Was Enuf.* Shange, criticized by some blacks for being anti-male, received praise from white male reviewers. As one friend commented to me sourly, "They don't think it's about them.") Even critics who long for new values in fiction (rather than simply new fiction embodying the old values) tend to look in the wrong places. An intelligent French Marxist, Gérard Klein, recently analyzed the pessimism of the last decade of American science fiction, finding it neither truthful nor politically honest, noticing "the absence of any Utopia, any social project" and stating that those who have "interiorized and accepted" the values which support the dominant group in a culture can convey or destroy those values, but only "the social and cultural peripheries are potentially capable to [sic] produce different, original values, values of the future."[9] I could not agree more. But where is the totally apposite, science-fictional counterexample Klein could have used: that raw, brilliant female Utopia published in 1969 by Klein's own feminist countrywoman, Monique Wittig? Where is *Les Guérillières?*

Nowhere, that's where. It is not even condemned. (As for Klein's sensitivity to other issues, he says of novelist Samuel

Delany, "there is only one Black SF writer in the U.S.A. and he could be held [sic] for a white one." One hopes Delany will disregard this piece of stereotyping.)

Instead the second part of Klein's article deals with the work of Ursula LeGuin, author of *The Dispossessed* and *The Left Hand of Darkness*, in which he finds "indirectly suggested what a female culture might be, acentric, tolerant, released . . . from the male cultural pattern of repetitive conquest." LeGuin can, he says, propose "a world without a central principle, without a unifying system, without domination, because she is a woman."

This is certainly praise, but the terms in which it's couched are reminiscent of the conventionally feminine virtues; later, in the same essay, Klein attributes LeGuin's artistic success to her nurturant qualities (Klein suggests that she reacted to the Freudian primal scene, in Klein's view the discovery of the existence of brothers and sisters—not Freud's view, as I remember—by installing "herself as mother"), the fact that her art is the product of "a happily resolved childhood, an active feminine genitality, and her intellectual indebtedness to her historian husband."[10] That is, the female artist is to be valued because she is motherly, happy, heterosexually mature, and influenced by her husband. Wittig, who is clearly (at least in her books) angry, discontented, lesbian, and in revolt against male influence, is not mentioned as the creator of new values. Nor does Klein appear to be aware of the indecency of making public statements about a living author's genitality—an indignity he visits only on the one woman in his two essays and not on any of the men, who are exempt from the psychosexual calculus by which he measures LeGuin's achievement.

Even a critic looking for new values recognizes them best when he can mistake them for old values, especially the old values for which he himself has a sentimental regard.

True, the old values are at the center. But the center is such a dead center. I think the sacred canon with its holy writ is really boring and frustrating its priests half to death; for one thing its texts are readable only if you are allowed to read them—i.e., see what's there, including the faults. And spending your whole lifetime with false universals can really do you in. I remember an intelligent, liberal professor in the early 1970s who once mentioned to me his disillusionment with literature. (He had carried his ideals so far as to teach in a nearby prison.) Didn't I think, said he, that reading was—well, a luxury? Wasn't there something idle and luxurious and really pretty trivial about just sitting in a room and reading a book?

And there I stood with my piccolo—I mean *Sexual Politics* and *Small Changes* (for starters) in my pockets.

Oh no, I said. No. Oh my God. Oh God, no.

Well, as in cells and sprouts, growth occurs only at the edges of something. From the peripheries, as Klein says. But even to see the peripheries, it seems, you have to be on them, or by an act of re-vision, place yourself there. Refining and strengthening the judgments you already have will get you nowhere. You must break set. It's either that or remain at the center. The dead, dead center.

I've been trying to finish this monster for thirteen ms. pages and it won't. Clearly it's not finished.

You finish it.

Author's Note

An as-yet-unpublished poet in Boulder, Colorado, once said to me that anything worth doing was worth doing badly. I may seem, in the foregoing sketchy pages, to have followed her advice rather too well. Yet one's choice in life is often between doing something partially and not doing it at all and the best choice is not necessarily the latter. A thorough investigation of the history of the suppression and discouragement of women's writing would take years of work and a good deal of money; lacking everything but the ambiguous leisure of a seven months' illness, I have attempted only to define those patterns which appear to me to have persisted for at least a century and a half and sometimes longer. The results of pulling together some of the feminist criticism done in this area during the last decade seem to me worthwhile: sometimes a dialogue between women who have never, in fact, met, sometimes an accumulation of examples to the point where a pattern emerges or a point is made. In fact, it is hard to stop accumulating evidence for this book, since the world so generously continues to provide it. If I have used examples from television productions a few times, it is partly because popular culture seems to me to provide a good illumination of high culture (being often derived from it but less sophisticated about mystifying our cultural assumptions) and partly because I do not regard the printed word as privileged. A responsible, dramatized biography is surely as citable as one written down— hence I have briefly used the life of Scott Joplin shown on

NBC-TV, assuming that the specific details of his professional career were reported accurately (though I would not swear to some of the personal life shown, for example the character of his wife, who was as Hollywooden as the heroine of the usual TV play). A fine example of false categorizing, which came to light after the book was completed, is the play *The Belle of Amherst*, mentioned by Adrienne Rich in her essay "Vesuvius at Home: The Power of Emily Dickinson."[1] The play repeats John Crowe Ransom's characterization of the poet as "a little home-keeping person" whose typography ought to be amended by the mature and professional commentator.

This work may stand as testimony to the hurriedness and peculiar "amateur" status of much feminist work of the last ten years. It's not that the authors are unskilled, but we must frequently venture outside our areas of original training. Either the work lies outside anybody's area of original training, or orthodox criticism (in Ellen Moers' words) averts its refined and weary eyes from what only feminists consider important or see as problematic. Much anti-feminist criticism of feminist writing can best be answered with, "Yeah? And where were you at the time, twinkletoes? Writing your ten-thousandth essay on *King Lear*?"

Perhaps the brachiopodal Glotolog will inspire someone to write a genuine history of the suppression, discouragement, and downgrading of women's writing or—God bless us! how Utopian can you get?—minority writing in general.

Until then I remain impenitent.

Seattle, 1978

Afterword

This Afterword is poetic justice.

There I was, with the other Glotologgi of my hue, slipping and sliding on the ice and frumenting like anything, while at the faraway periphery of our Great, Classical, Normal, Serious, and totally Central circle loomed (but faintly) dim and disquieting shapes. Some were (irresponsibly) not-Serious; some were (shame!) not-Normal, some (inexplicably) not-Classical, and all of them (indubitably) not-Great.

They were, after all, outside the Circle.

Of course we were fair-minded, and would have instantly let into the Circle (which was also Immortal, by the way) any who demonstrated Circular qualities, as long as they were just like ours.

Somehow they were not.

We did, actually, let a few in. (This made us feel generous.)

Most, we did not. (This made us feel that we had high and important standards.)

Some didn't even want to get in and stood about making rude remarks. (This made us feel scared.)

But how on earth could we possibly let them in?

They were clumsy.

Their work was thin.

It wasn't about the right things.

It was *subsidiary*.

It had no "universal values." (These are shiny gold bells, worn on the head, which are indispensable to the art of frument, and which the practicing frumentor, by shaking the head back and forth, causes to go "bing! bing!" in complicated rhythmic outbursts while performing the other actions proper to this delicate and complex art.)

To drop the metaphor (which is four years old by now and showing a bit of wear and tear), when white critic Elly Bulkin informed a roomful of us white feminists (at the university in which I teach) that we were racists and homophobes, I felt both angry and accused. After all, none of us had done anything that bad and we were hardly responsible for the Great Tradition of English literature being largely white, or that others were subsidiary, or that so little had been done in these latter. I had certainly confronted homosexuality in women's writing, no matter what other literary feminists had done, and so would I confront color—when and where it was appropriate to do so, of course.

To prove all this, I went to the library, got Black novelist Zora Neale Hurston's classic, *Their Eyes Were Watching God*,[1] and read it.

It was episodic.

It was thin.

It was uninteresting.

The characters talked funny.

It was clearly inferior to the great central tradition of Western Literature (if you added these authors' wives', mothers', daughters', sisters', and colleagues' books). I'd been vindicated. Why go on?

But Elly must have put a virus in my tea or otherwise affected me, as shortly thereafter I returned from the library with one armful of books and from the bookstore with another, all these about women of color. There were novels, short-story collections, books containing literary criticism, literary journals, and a few slender pamphlets from small presses. Then I read John Langston Gwaltney's *Drylongso*,[2] Gerda Lerner's *Black Women in White America,*[3] Barbara Christian's pioneering study *Black Women Novelists,*[4] *Conditions: Five, the Black Women's Issue,*[5] Toni Cade Bambara's *The Black Woman: An Anthology,*[6] Mary Helen Washington's *Black-Eyed Susans: Classic Stories by and about Black Women,*[7] and Barbara Smith's *Toward a Black Feminist Criticism.*[8]

Then I reread *Their Eyes Were Watching God.*

It was astonishing how much the novel had improved in the interval.

Could it be that all these authors were not—as I had unthinkingly assumed—in subsidiary traditions, but *parallel ones?* And that the only thing unique, superior to all others, and especially important in my tradition, was that I was in it? Was centrality really a relative matter?

It's very difficult to convey to others that sudden access of light, that soundless blow, that changes forever one's map of the world. After complaining about exclusivity from the victim's viewpoint, I had then spent four years as a cultural solipsist myself, and what was worse, I went on to do more of the same. Extracting a few pages' more space from my editor, I started to read (this was the one right thing I did, actually). It couldn't be really that much of a project, and a fairly accurate—though of course somewhat sketchy—essay about women writers of color would enhance my book wonderfully.

Happily, I took notes.

I read.

I thought.

I had planned to consult with a Black colleague, but when I approached her in the hall she had a crowd of students about, all of them talking, a stack of books in one arm, a mass of student papers in the other, seven committee reports wedged in between, as well as her small daughter in a backpack, and she was looking surreptitiously at her watch. So I went on reading and taking notes.

It was all great fun.

Then a deadline loomed, and I sat down to consult my notes—most of them direct quotations.

There were 250 of them.

With an increased respect for my scholarly colleagues, who deal with such things all the time (I once asked a young dissertation writer whether her suddenly grayed hair was due to ill health or personal tragedy; she answered *It was the footnotes*), I set aside all my nineteenth-century material, everything not written or said by a novelist, poet, etc., most of my quotations from well-known authors, and every public, impersonal statement by anybody. I then put the remaining quotations into categories, thus: Racism (37), Sexism (21), Homophobia (11), Class and Money (14), Racism in the Women's Movement (a whopping 21), Education (15), Prejudice in Publishing and Reviewing (10), Models and Support Systems (a heartening 27), Mothers and Grandmothers (a lovely category, 14), and Bilingualism and Love of Language (26).

Even thus reduced, the quotations numbered 196, and would add quite a bit to my manuscript all by themselves, let alone all the other stuff I was supposed to write. Worse still, my choice of quotations had made the authors sound as if they did nothing but suffer and weep, from time to time producing soggy mss. all about the aforesaid weeping, etc. Worse still, the material refused to be structured no matter what organizational principles I dreamed up. My invented categories were clearly inadequate and any other structure that did justice to the stuff instantly introduced six subjects for each one I had begun with and demanded excursions into history, psychology, economics, and politics, while interconnections proliferated with the speed of the carnivorous flora in horror movies. It was like trying to put the Atlantic Ocean in a teacup.

Who had said *what* about *which* other whole traditions?

Dammit (I decided then), I'll print only the quotations themselves, all 196 of them.

Then I thought: *196 more footnotes* . . .

And that's when I broke down.

As I was going under the sea of index cards for the third time, somehow sanity reasserted itself. *Why on earth* (said a still, small voice) *do you want to describe the conditions of work and life for women writers of color when they are doing so perfectly well themselves, and better, in fact, than you ever can?*

What you should do (it continued) *is share with other readers who may not know these writers, some of their energy, their talent, and their love of language.*

Here is my own eccentric, idiosyncratic, incomplete list of things that somehow stuck with me. (I have eight novels and three anthologies to go, just in this batch.) Enjoy, enjoy.

Where are the people who say *I am, I am* as the gulls do?

CHRYSTOS, "No Rock Scorns Me as Whore"[9]

Octavia Butler's wild and talented science fiction novels.[10]

The highly ethical singer-heroine of Jewelle Gomez's charming story—who is a vampire ("No Day Too Long").[11]

I'm not invincible, I tell you. My skin's as fragile as a baby's I'm brittle bones and human, I tell you. I'm a broken arm./ You're a razor's edge, you tell me. Shock them shitless. Be the holocaust. Be the black Kali. Spit in their eye and never cry. Oh broken angel . . . be not a rock but a razor's edge and burn with falling.

GLORIA ANZALDÚA, "La Prieta"[12]

Snapping little dark eyes, skin the color of well-buttered cara-
mel, and a body like the Venus of Willendorf. Ginger was gor-
geously fat . . . delicate and precise. Her breasts were high and
ample, and she had pads of firm fat upon her thighs, and round
dimpled knees. Her swift tapered hands and little feet . . .

AUDRE LORDE, "The Beginning"[13]

The clouds take shape, white trout, slow-moving cats . . .

LINDA HOGAN, "Sophie"[14]

[Fantasized, as a 15-year-old] . . . when the starships returned,
they would all be driven by black women, seven feet tall, land-
ing and reducing to rubbish all the earth's ammunition and
the bishop of our church to fly shit. I imagined . . . all of the
church women getting naughty winks from Amazons . . .

PAT SUNCIRCLE, "A Day's Growth"[15]

billie lives! billie lives!
    . . . she's probably got a little house somewhere with
yemany jezabel the queen of Sheba . . . sojourner truth ma
rainey ida cox lil hardin and sapphire & her mama. . . . [Bil-
lie Holliday made a tape that had] those bigtime bigdaddies
jumpin outta windows and otherwise offin theyselves. . . .
it was one of those my man is dead so now i am gonna
throw myself in his grave too funeral dirge numbers (tragic
mulatress division). . . . [Billie] turned it around on them. . . .
[if you, the reader, think she was unaware of what she was
doing, confused and heartbroken—] nigguh, pullease!
well but if you think like that then you don't belong in this

poem so i am gonna cancel you right out. go somewhere and
write yo own poem.

HATTIE GOSSET, "billie lives! billie lives!"[16]

... how I spoke was a linguist's treat ... yiddish and spanish
and fine refined college educated english and irish which I
mainly keep in my prayers. . . . I spoke mockDickens and
mockBritish. . . . I really really dig the funny way the British
speak ... and i love too the singing of yiddish sentences. . . .
oh and those words hundreds of them dotting the english
language like raisins in the bread ...

ROSARIO MORALES, "I Am What I Am"[17]

(On lack of time)

I was able to snatch a few precious days in the month of January in which to write undisturbed. But ... when shall I ever
be so fortunate again as to break a foot?

FLORENCE PRICE, in *Some of Us Were Brave*[18]

(Actually Florence Price is a composer, but I couldn't resist;
this seems to be the ultimate comment on the subject.)

(About grandmothers)

> I write my check to the heart fund.
> I remember how she puffed
> up the stairs with pancakes
> she made for our lunch

when we moved across the hall.
Light. Golden.

NELLIE WONG, "Grandmothers"[19]

(After the difficult death of her grandmother in hospital)

Last night I dreamt I was in a wide open space. A rolling
countryside all white like it was covered with snow, and I felt
really peaceful. It wasn't cold either. I blew air onto my hands
and didn't see its trace in front of me. As I walked, I saw Poa
Poa [Grandmother] standing in the snow smiling at me.
She was glowing. Then, I saw a bright light coming out of her
mouth with each exhale.

My Poa Poa is living. My Poa Poa is living, breathing light.

KITTY TSUI, "Poa Poa Is Living Breathing Light"[20]

(And so many mothers)

... when my mother is working in her flowers ... she is radi-
ant almost to the point of being invisible—except as Creator: hand and eye.

ALICE WALKER, "In Search of Our Mothers' Gardens"[21]

I remember all of my mother's stories. . . . She is a fine story-
teller, recalling every event of her life with the vividness of
the present, noting each detail right down to the cut and
color of her dress.

CHERRIE MORAGA, "La Guera"[22]

(Also)

When entering a room full of soldiers who fear hearts you put your heart in your back pocket.

MORAGA, "Anatomy Lesson"[23]

Her grandma ... was one for stories ... [about] everything that ever happened to the Alvarado Family. . . . there must have been at least a thousand (characters). . . . It was like watching someone weave a blanket right there under your very nose.

JO CARRILLO, "Maria Littlebear"[24]

Night after night my mother would talk-story until we fell asleep. I couldn't tell where the stories left off and the dreams began, her voice the voice of the heroines in my sleep.

MAXINE HONG KINGSTON, *The Woman Warrior*[25]

Picture a large, old-fashioned kitchen with a secondhand refrigerator, the kind they used to have back in the thirties with a motor on top, a coal stove that in its blackness, girth, and the heat it threw off during the winter overwhelmed the gas range next to it, a sink whose pipes never ceased their rusty cough, and a large table covered with flowered oilcloth set like an altar in the middle of the room. . . . my mother and her friends (after a working day spent cleaning white women's houses) would there in the sanctuary of our kitchen, talk endlessly, passionately. . . . The people they worked for were usually the first thing to come under the whiplash of their tongues ...

For me, listening in a corner of the kitchen (seen but not heard, as was the rule back then), it wasn't only what the women talked about . . . it was their poet's skill with words. They had taken the language imposed on them and imbued it with their own incisive rhythms and syntax, brought to bear upon it the few African words that had been retained. . . . They didn't know it, nor did I at the time, but they were carrying on a tradition as ancient as Africa . . .

PAULE MARSHALL, "Shaping the World of My Art"[26]

(What is there about mothers and kitchens? I used to stand just outside the door of ours, my friend Susan Koppelman sat *under* the kitchen table, careful not to move, and Marge Piercy has a poem about being—not literally, though—a bump under the kitchen tablecloth.)

Barbara Smith and Beverly Smith, "Homophobia in the Black Community," in "Across the Kitchen Table, a Sister-Sister Dialogue."[27]

A new press for the writings of women of color in New York City called Kitchen Table Press.[28]

. . . momma
help me
turn the face of history
to your face.

JUNE JORDAN, "Getting Down to Get Over,
Dedicated to My Mother,"[29]

. . . if we were to have lots and lots of them (stories) from Indian women there would be . . . beauty . . . *pride*, the feeling that comes from watching the stream of black-birds traveling in the fall, unable to see the beginning or the ending, just many, many, passing overhead, hearing their voices.

FLYING CLOUDS, Biographical Note
Lesbian Fiction[30]
Seattle, 1982

Notes

1. PROHIBITIONS

1. James Baldwin, "My Dungeon Shook: Letter to My Nephew on the One Hundredth Anniversary of the Emancipation," in *The Fire Next Time* (New York: Dell, 1964), p. 21.

2. Virginia Woolf, *Three Guineas* (New York: Harcourt, Brace & World, 1938), p. 75.

3. Ellen Moers, *Literary Women* (Garden City: Anchor Press/Doubleday, 1977), p. 181.

4. M. Jeanne Peterson, "The Victorian Governess: Status Incongruence in Family and Society," in *Suffer and Be Still: Women in the Victorian Age*, ed. Martha Vicinus (Bloomington: Indiana University Press, 1972), p. 8.

5. Virginia Woolf, *A Room of One's Own* (New York: Harcourt, Brace & World, 1929), p. 73.

6. Gordon S. Haight, *George Eliot: A Biography* (Oxford University Press, 1968), pp. 66, 295.

7. Eve Curie, *Madame Curie: A Biography*, trans. Vincent Sheean (Garden City: Doubleday, Doran, 1937), pp. 138, 143–144, 150.

8. Tillie Olsen, "Silences: When Writers Don't Write," in *Images of Women in Fiction: Feminist Perspectives*, ed. Susan Koppelman Cornillon (Bowling Green: Bowling Green University Popular Press, 1972), pp. 109–110.

9. Cited by Tillie Olsen, in *Silences* (New York: Delacorte Press/Seymour Lawrence, 1978), p. 18.

10. Tillie Olsen, "A Biographical Interpretation," appendix to *Life in the Iron Mills; or, the Korl Woman*, by Rebecca Harding Davis (Old Westbury: The Feminist Press, 1972).

11. Kate Wilhelm, "Women Writers: A Letter from Kate Wilhelm," *The Witch and the Chameleon* 3 (April 1975): 21–22.

12. Karen Petersen and J. J. Wilson, *Women Artists: Recognition and Reappraisal from the Early Middle Ages to the Twentieth Century* (New York: Harper & Row, 1976), pp. 44, 84, 85.

13. Cited by Woolf, in *A Room of One's Own*, pp. 62, 65.

14. Cited by Elizabeth Gaskell, in *Life of Charlotte Brontë* (London, 1919), pp. 102, 104.

15. Ellen Glasgow, *The Woman Within* (New York: Harcourt, Brace, 1954), pp. 62, 63, 65.

16. Gordon S. Haight, ed., *A Century of George Eliot Criticism* (Boston: Houghton Mifflin, 1965), p. 144.

17. Florence Howe, "Literacy and Literature," *PMLA* 89, no. 3 (1974): 438.

18. Florence Howe, "Varieties of Denial," *Colloquy* 6, no. 9 (November 1973): 3.

19. Elizabeth Pochoda, "Heroines," in *Woman: An Issue*, ed. Lee R. Edwards, Mary Heath, and Lisa Baskin (New York: Little, Brown, 1972), p. 179.

20. Jo Freeman, "How to Discriminate against Women without Really Trying" (Pittsburgh: K.N.O.W. #03306, n.d.), p. 1.

21. Wilhelm, "Women Writers," p. 21.

22. Chelsea Quinn Yarbro in *Khatru* 3 & 4 (November 1975), ed. Jeffrey Smith (Baltimore: Phantasmicon Press Publication #41), p. 110.

23. Personal interview with Phyllis Chesler, summer 1977.

24. Yarbro, *Khatru*, p. 110.

25. J. J. Wilson, "So You Mayn't Ever Call Me Anything but Carrington," in *Woman: An Issue*, ed. Edwards et al., p. 293.

26. Anaïs Nin, *The Diary of Anaïs Nin*, ed. Gunther Stuhlmann (New York: Harcourt, Brace & World, 1966), 1:291.

27. Yarbro, *Khatru*, p. 52.

28. Lee R. Edwards, "Women, Energy, and *Middlemarch*," in *Woman: An Issue*, ed. Edwards et al., pp. 227–229.

29. Adrienne Rich, "When We Dead Awaken: Writing as Re-vision," *College English* 34, no. 1 (October 1972): 21.

30. Samuel Delany, *Khatru*, p. 28.

31. Suzanne Juhasz, *Naked and Fiery Forms: Modern American Poetry by Women, A New Tradition* (New York: Harper & Row, 1976), pp. 88–89, 103.

32. Sylvia Plath, *Ariel* (New York: Harper & Row, 1965), p. 84.

33. Rich, "When We Dead Awaken," pp. 21–22.

34. Quoted by Barbara Kevles, in "The Art of Poetry: Anne Sexton," *Paris Review* 13 (1970–71): 160.

2. BAD FAITH

1. Abraham Maslow, *Motivation and Personality* (New York: Harper, 1954), p. 270.

3. DENIAL OF AGENCY

1. Virginia Woolf, "The Duchess of Newcastle," in *The Common Reader* (New York: Harcourt, Brace, 1925), p. 75.

2. Petersen and Wilson, *Women Artists*, pp. 53, 56, 58.

3. Ibid., J. J. Wilson, lecture given at the University of Colorado, Boulder, 1976.

4. Stella Gibbons, *Cold Comfort Farm* (New York: Penguin Books, 1977).

5. Cited by Carol Ohmann, in "Emily Brontë in the Hands of Male Critics," *College English* 32, no. 8 (May 1971): 907.

6. Moers, *Literary Women*, p. 144.

7. Ohmann, "Emily Brontë in the Hands of Male Critics," pp. 909–910.

8. Cited by Haight, in *A Century of George Eliot Criticism*, p. 168.

9. Haight, *George Eliot: A Biography*, p. 29.

10. Mary Ellmann, *Thinking about Women* (New York: Harcourt Brace Jovanovich, 1968), pp. 41–42.

11. Colette, *The Pure and the Impure*, trans. Herma Briffault (New York: Farrar, Straus & Giroux, 1966), pp. 59–63.

12. Ursula LeGuin, *Khatru*, p. 16.

13. Letter received from Sonya Dorman, 5 December 1970.

14. Charles Dickens, *Letters of Charles Dickens*, ed. Madeline House and Graham Storey (Oxford: Clarendon Press, 1965), p. 263.

15. Robert Lowell, foreword to *Ariel*, by Sylvia Plath, p. vii.

16. Delany, *Khatru*, pp. 74–75.

17. Yarbro, *Khatru*, p. 55.

4. POLLUTION OF AGENCY

1. Charlotte Brontë, *Villette* (London: The Zodiac Press, 1967), pp. 251–253.

2. George Bernard Shaw, *Our Theatres in the Nineties* (London: Constable, 1932), 3:274, 276–277, 295.

3. Elaine Showalter, "Women Writers and the Double Standard," in *Woman in Sexist Society: Studies in Power and Powerlessness*, ed. Vivian Gornick and Barbara K. Moran (New York: New American Library, 1972), pp. 476–477, 475, 457, 456.

4. Louis Simpson, "New Books of Poems," *Harper's*, August 1967, p. 91.

5. Dolores Palomo, "A Woman Writer and the Scholars: A Review of Mary Manley's Reputation," *Woman and Literature* 6, no. 1 (Spring 1978): 41, 38–39.

6. Julia Penelope [Stanley], "Fear of *Flying?*," *Sinister Wisdom* 1, no. 2 (December 1976): 54–55, 62.

7. Lowell, foreword to *Ariel*, p. vii.

8. Cited by Moers, in *Literary Women*, p. 22.

9. Cited by Showalter, in "Women Writers and the Double Standard," pp. 466–467.

10. Olga Broumas, *Beginning with O* (New Haven: Yale University Press, 1977).

11. Phyllis Chesler, *About Men* (New York: Simon & Schuster, 1978), pp. 106–107.

12. In *By a Woman Writt*, ed. Joan Goulianos (Baltimore: Penguin, 1974), p. 137.

13. Cited by Eva Figes, in *Patriarchal Attitudes* (New York: Fawcett, 1971), p. 95.

14. Cited by Moers, in *Literary Women*, p. 271.

15. Moers, *Literary Women*, p. 281.

16. Cited by Showalter, in "Women Writers and the Double Standard," p. 453.

17. Dick Brukenfeld, "Theatre: Three by Russ," *The Village Voice*, 2 October 1969, p. 45.

18. Elaine Reuben, "Can a Young Girl from a Small Mining Town Find Happiness Writing Criticism for *The New York Review of Books?*" *College English* 34, no. 1 (October 1972): 40–43. Reuben quotes Podhoretz.

NOTES TO PAGES 42–57   183

19. Quoted by Figes, in *Patriarchal Attitudes*, pp. 129, 143–144, 148.
20. Elizabeth Janeway, *Man's World, Woman's Place* (New York: Dell, 1971), p. 109.
21. Marya Mannes, *New York Times Book Review*, 13 August 1967, p. 17.
22. Marya Mannes, "Problems of Creative Women," in *Up Against the Wall, Mother* . . . , ed. Elsie Adams and Mary Louise Briscoe (Beverly Hills: Glencoe Press, 1971), pp. 402–415.
23. Tillie Olsen, "Women Who Are Writers in Our Century: One Out of Twelve," *College English* 34, no. 1 (October 1972): 9, 10.
24. In *By a Woman Writt*, ed. Goulianos, pp. 270–271.
25. Janeway, *Man's World, Woman's Place*, p. 109.

5. THE DOUBLE STANDARD OF CONTENT

1. Reuben, "Can a Young Girl," p. 41.
2. Mary McCarthy, *Theatre Chronicles* (New York: The Noonday Press, 1968), pp. ix–x.
3. Woolf, *A Room of One's Own*, pp. 76–77.
4. Ellmann, *Thinking about Women*, p. 92.
5. Chesler, *About Men*, pp. 211–212.
6. Woolf, *A Room of One's Own*, p. 73.
7. Cited by Haight, in *A Century of George Eliot Criticism*, p. 204.
8. Judith Fetterley, talk given at MLA convention, December 1975.
9. Ohmann, "Emily Brontë in the Hands of Male Critics," pp. 907–912.
10. Robert Silverberg, "Who Is Tiptree, What Is He?," in *Warm Worlds and Otherwise* by James Tiptree Jr. (New York: Ballantine Books, 1975), pp. xii–xv, xviii.
11. Cited by Ohmann, in "Emily Brontë in the Hands of Male Critics," p. 907.
12. Suzy McKee Charnas, *Khatru*, pp. 86–87.
13. Stephen Spender, "Warnings from the Grave," *New Republic*, 8 June 1966, p. 26.
14. Ellmann, *Thinking about Women*, p. 85.
15. Delany, *Khatru*, p. 33.
16. Moers, *Literary Women*, p. xiv.

6. FALSE CATEGORIZING

1. Margaret Mead, *Male and Female* (New York: Morrow, 1949), pp. 257–258.

2. Petersen and Wilson, *Women Artists*, pp. 8, 20, 95, 89, 166–167.

3. Cynthia Fuchs Epstein, "Sex Role Stereotyping, Occupations, and Social Exchange," *Women's Studies* 3 (1976): 190, 193–194.

4. Charnas, *Khatru*, p. 107.

5. Vonda McIntyre, *Khatru*, p. 120.

6. Harold Clurman, "It Was a People's Theatre," *TV Guide*, 18 February 1978, p. 33.

7. Moers, *Literary Women*, pp. 225, 227–228.

8. "Scott Joplin: King of Ragtime," NBC-TV, 20 June 1978.

9. W. H. Auden and Norman Holmes Pearson, eds., *Poets of the English Language* (New York: The Viking Press, 1953), p. v.

10. Woolf, *A Room of One's Own*, p. 65.

11. Personal interview with Dolores Palomo, summer 1978.

12. Louis Untermeyer, ed., *A Treasury of Great Poems, English and American* (New York: Simon & Schuster, 1942).

13. Helene Moglen, *Charlotte Brontë: The Self Conceived* (New York: W. W. Norton, 1976), p. 241.

7. ISOLATION

1. Petersen and Wilson, *Women Artists*, pp. 9, 7, 166.

2. Mary Shelley, *The Last Man* (Lincoln: University of Nebraska Press, 1965).

3. Cited by Moers, in *Literary Women*, p. 19.

4. Virginia Woolf, "Aurora Leigh," in *The Second Common Reader* (New York: Harcourt, Brace, 1932), pp. 185–192.

5. Kate Millet, *Sexual Politics* (New York: Avon, 1971), pp. 192–202.

6. Moers, *Literary Women*, pp. 163ff.

7. Millet, *Sexual Politics*, pp. 192, 200.

8. Claudia Van Gerven, "Lost Literary Traditions: A Matter of Influence," MS, p. 2.

9. Jean S. Mullen, "Freshman Textbooks," *College English* 34, no. 1 (October 1972): 79–80.

10. Woolf, *Three Guineas*, pp. 146, 18, 12–13.

11. Jane Marcus, "Art and Anger," *Feminist Studies* 4, no. 1 (February 1978): 81, 87.

12. Woolf, *Three Guineas*, p. 109. So did Margaret Cavendish, Duchess of Newcastle. An ardent Royalist, she nonetheless wrote in one of her "Sociable Letters" (actually a form of fiction): "We are not tied nor bound to state or Crown. We are free, not sworn to allegiance, nor do we take the oath of Supremacy. . . . And if we be not citizens in the commonwealth, I know no reason we should be subjects to the commonwealth." She adds that "though there has been a civil war in the kingdom, and a general war amongst the men, yet there has been none against the women. They have not fought pitched battles . . . and . . . her Ladyship is the same in my affection, as if the kingdom had been in a calm peace" (in *By a Woman Writt*, ed. Goulianos, pp. 61–62).

13. Marcus, "Art and Anger," p. 88.

14. Woolf, *A Room of One's Own*, pp. 94, 111.

15. Berenice A. Carroll, "'To Crush Him in Our Own Country': The Political Thought of Virginia Woolf," *Feminist Studies* 4, no. 1 (February 1978): 104, 115–116, 120, 123.

16. Ibid., pp. 130, 131, 104, 105.

17. Woolf, *A Room of One's Own*, pp. 37–38.

18. Herbert Marder, *Feminism and Art: A Study of Virginia Woolf* (Chicago: University of Chicago Press, 1968), p. 175.

19. Quentin Bell, *Virginia Woolf A Biography* (New York: Harcourt Brace Jovanovich, 1972), 2:204.

20. Marcus, "Art and Anger," p. 88.

21. Carroll, "The Political Thought of Virginia Woolf," p. 99.

22. Marder, *Feminism and Art*, p. 23.

23. Carroll, "The Political Thought of Virginia Woolf," p. 119.

24. Marcus, "Art and Anger," pp. 93–94.

25. Ibid., p. 81.

26. Ibid., pp. 81ff.

8. ANOMALOUSNESS

1. F. T. Palgrave's *The Golden Treasury of the Best Songs and Lyrical Poems: Centennial Edition*, ed. Oscar Williams (New York: New American Library, 1961), pp. viii, xi, ix.

2. Van Gerven, "Lost Literary Traditions," p. 2.

3. Frederick O. Waage, "Urban Broadsides of Renaissance England," *Journal of Popular Culture* 11, no. 3 (Winter 1977): 736.

4. Mullen, "Freshman Textbooks," p. 79.

5. Elaine Showalter, "Women and the Literary Curriculum," *College English* 32, no. 8 (May 1971): 856.

6. Van Gerven, "Lost Literary Traditions," pp. 2–3, 5–6.

7. Cited by Juhasz, in *Naked and Fiery Forms*, p. 11.

8. *Ibid.*, p. 9.

9. Moers, *Literary Women*, pp. 83, 85–86, 87, 91–92.

10. Juhasz, *Naked and Fiery Forms*, p. 7.

11. Van Gerven, "Lost Literary Traditions," p. 4.

12. Juhasz, *Naked and Fiery Forms*, pp. 7–9.

13. Van Gerven, "Lost Literary Traditions," p. 5.

14. Virginia Woolf, "Geraldine and Jane," in *The Second Common Reader*, pp. 167–181.

15. Natalie Barney, "Natalie Barney on Renée Vivien," trans. Margaret Porter, *Heresies* 3 (Fall 1977): 71.

16. Blanche Weisen Cook, "Female Support Networks and Political Activism," *Chrysalis* 3 (1977): 45–46.

17. Moers, *Literary Women*, pp. 87, 66, 208, 211.

18. Personal interview with Dolores Palomo, summer 1978.

19. Judith Long Laws, "The Psychology of Tokenism: An Analysis," *Sex Roles* 1, no. 1 (1975): 51.

20. Samuel Delany, "To Read the Dispossessed," in *The Jewel-Hinged Jaw* (New York: Berkley, 1978), p. 261.

21. Audre Lorde, *The New York Head Shop and Museum* (Detroit: Broadside, 1974), p. 48.

22. In *By a Woman Writt*, ed. Goulianos, p. 92.

9. LACK OF MODELS

1. Showalter, "Women and the Literary Curriculum," p. 855.

2. Florence Howe, "Identity and Expression: A Writing Course for Women," *College English* 32, no. 8 (May 1971): 863.

3. Letter received from Marilyn Hacker, 17 November 1976.

4. Association of American Colleges, *On Campus with Women: Project on the Status and Education of Women*, #20 (Washington, DC: June 1978), p. 1.

5. Erica Jong, "The Artist as Housewife," in *The First Ms. Reader*, ed. Francine Klagsbrun (New York: Warner Paperback Library, 1973), pp. 116–117.

6. Quoted by Elly Bulkin, in "An Interview with Adrienne Rich," *Conditions* 2 (1977): 54–55.

7. Untermeyer, ed., *A Treasury of Great Poems*, p. 941.

8. Quoted by Virginia Woolf, in "I Am Christina Rossetti," in *The Second Common Reader*, pp. 218–219.

9. Ibid., pp. 219, 215.

10. Cynthia Ozick, "Women and Creativity: The Demise of the Dancing Dog," in *Woman in Sexist Society*, ed. Gornick and Moran, pp. 434–435.

11. Ferdinand Lundberg and Marynia Farnham, *Modern Woman: The Lost Sex* (New York: Harper & Brothers, 1947).

12. Millet, *Sexual Politics*, pp. 278–281.

13. Marcus, "Art and Anger," p. 73.

14. Woolf, *A Room of One's Own*, p. 98.

15. Linda Nochlin, "Why Are There No Great Woman Artists?," in *Woman in Sexist Society*, ed. Gornick and Moran, p. 483.

16. Juhasz, *Naked and Fiery Forms*, p. 1.

17. Woolf, "Aurora Leigh," pp. 182–192.

10. RESPONSES

1. Personal interview with Dolores Palomo, summer 1978.

2. Jeffrey Smith, *Khatru*, pp. 53, 109.

3. Cited by Ozick, in "Women and Creativity," pp. 446, 431, 448.

4. Cited by Reuben, in "Can a Young Girl," p. 44.

5. Olsen, "A Biographical Interpretation," in *Life in the Iron Mills*, pp. 138, 135, 140, 144, 145.

6. Alice Quinn, review of *Simone Weil: A Life*, by Simone Petrémont, *Chrysalis* 3 (1977): 121, 120.

7. Marcus, "Art and Anger," p. 93.

8. Juhasz, *Naked and Fiery Forms*, p. 39.

9. Ellmann, *Thinking about Women*, pp. 199, 210, 229.

10. Woolf, *A Room of One's Own*, p. 78.

11. Jane Austen, *Northanger Abbey* (London: Franklin Watts, Ltd., 1971), pp. 30–32.

12. In *By a Woman Writt*, ed. Goulianos, p. 99.

13. Margaret Cavendish, Duchess of Newcastle, "To the Reader," in *The Description of a New World Called the Blazing World* (London: A. Maxwell, 1668).

14. In *By a Woman Writt*, ed. Goulianos, p. 291.

15. Louise Fishman, ed., "The Tapes," *Heresies* 3 (Fall 1977): 18.

16. Jehanne H. Teilhet, "The Equivocal Role of Women Artists in Non-Literate Cultures," *Heresies* 4 (Winter 1978): 98.

17. Brontë, *Villette*, p. 74.

18. Cited by Moers, in *Literary Women*, p. 171.

19. Margaret Cavendish, Duchess of Newcastle, "Dedicatory Letters," in *Philosophical and Physical Opinions* (n.p., 1663), pp. 6–8.

20. In *By a Woman Writt*, ed. Goulianos, p. 72.

21. Alexandra Kollontai, *The Autobiography of a Sexually Emancipated Communist Woman, Alexandra Kollontai*, ed. Irving Fetscher (New York: Herder & Herder, 1971), p. 111.

22. Quoted by Cook, in "Female Support Networks," p. 58.

23. Yi-tsi Feuerwerker, "Ting Ling's 'When I Was in Sha Chuan (Cloud Village),'" *Signs: Journal of Women in Culture and Society* 2, no. 1 (1976): 277, 278.

24. In *By a Woman Writt*, ed. Goulianos, p. 24.

25. Woolf, *A Room of One's Own*, p. 108.

26. Cited by Marcus, in "Art and Anger," pp. 83, 85.

27. Cited by Carroll, "The Political Thought of Virginia Woolf," p. 102.

28. Marcus, "Art and Anger," p. 95.

29. Cited by Woolf, in *A Room of One's Own*, p. 64.

30. Moers, *Literary Women*, pp. 26, 24.

31. Cited by Goulianos, in *By a Woman Writt*, p. xv.

32. Letter received from Marilyn Hacker, 18 June 1977.

33. Judy Chicago, *Through the Flower: My Life as a Woman Artist* (Garden City: Doubleday, 1975), p. 154.

34. Moers, *Literary Women*, pp. xviii, xix, xx.

35. Bertha Harris, *Lover* (Plainfield, VT: Daughters, Inc., 1976).

36. Woolf, *A Room of One's Own*, pp. 85–86.

37. Moers, *Literary Women*, p. 3.

NOTES TO PAGES 135–147   189

11. AESTHETICS

1. Carolyn Kizer, "Pro Femina," in *No More Masks,* ed. Ellen Bass and Florence Howe (Garden City: Doubleday, 1973), p. 175.

2. Jean Baker Miller, *Toward a New Psychology of Women* (Boston: Beacon Press, 1975), pp. 47, 120, 8.

3. Lillian S. Robinson, "Who's Afraid of a Room of One's Own?," in *The Politics of Literature: Dissenting Essays on the Teaching of English,* ed. Louis Kampf and Paul Lauter (New York: Random House, 1973), pp. 376–377.

4. Annis Pratt, "The New Feminist Criticism," *College English* 32, no. 8 (May 1971): 877.

5. Lillian S. Robinson, "Dwelling in Decencies: Radical Criticism and the Feminist Perspective," *College English* 32, no. 8 (May 1971): 884–887.

6. Dolores Barracano Schmidt, "The Great American Bitch," *College English* 32, no. 8 (May 1971): 904.

7. Cynthia Griffin Wolff, "A Mirror for Men: Stereotypes of Women in Literature," in *Woman: An Issue,* ed. Edwards et al., pp. 207–208, 217.

8. Judith Fetterley, MLA convention, December 1975, pp. 8–9.

9. McIntyre, *Khatru,* p. 119.

10. Ellen Cantarow, "Why Teach Literature?" in *The Politics of Literature,* ed. Kampf and Lauter, pp. 57–61.

11. Mary D. Garrard, "Feminism: Has It Changed Art History?" *Heresies* 4 (1978): 60.

12. Valerie Jaudon and Joyce Kozloff, "Art Hysterical Notions of Progress and Culture," *Heresies* 4 (1978): 38–42.

13. Adrienne Rich, *Poems: Selected and New, 1950–1974* (New York: W. W. Norton, 1975), pp. 205–206.

14. In *By a Woman Writt,* ed. Goulianos, p. 99.

15. Adrienne Rich, "Conditions for Work: The Common World of Women," *Heresies* 3 (1977): 53–54.

16. Juhasz, *Naked and Fiery Forms,* pp. 139, 178–179.

17. Penelope, "Fear of *Flying?*" p. 59.

18. Juhasz, *Naked and Fiery Forms,* pp. 185, 201.

19. Virginia Woolf, *To the Lighthouse* (New York: Harcourt, Brace & World, 1927), p. 15.

20. Juhasz, *Naked and Fiery Forms,* p. 201.

21. Chicago, *Through the Flower,* p. 127.

EPILOGUE

1. Cited by Moers, in *Literary Women*, p. 66.

2. Personal interview with Dolores Palomo, summer 1978.

3. H. Bruce Franklin, "The Teaching of Literature in the Highest Academies of the Empire," in *The Politics of Literature*, ed. Kampf and Lauter, pp. 101–129.

4. Harold Beaver, introduction to *Billy Budd, Sailor and Other Stories*, by Herman Melville (Baltimore: Penguin Books, 1967), p. 18.

5. Kathi Maio, "(Skeleton in the) Closet Literature: A Look at Women's Mystery Fiction," *The Second Wave* 4, no. 4 (Summer/Fall 1976): 11–13.

6. Margaret Irwin, "The Book," in *The Satanists*, ed. Peter Haining (New York: Taplinger, 1970).

7. E. F. Bleiler, introduction to *Best Ghost Stories of J. S. LeFanu*, by J[oseph] S[heridan] LeFanu (New York: Dover Publications, 1964), p. v.

8. Cited by Maio, in "(Skeleton in the) Closet Literature," p. 9.

9. Gérard Klein, "Discontent in American Science Fiction," trans. D. Suvin and Leila Lecorps, *Science-Fiction Studies* 4, no. 1 (March 1977): 12, 13.

10. Gérard Klein, "Le Guin's 'Aberrant' Opus: Escaping the Trap of Discontent," *Science-Fiction Studies* 4, no. 3 (November 1977): 291–295.

AUTHOR'S NOTE

1. Adrienne Rich, "Vesuvius at Home: The Power of Emily Dickinson," in *On Lies, Secrets, and Silence: Selected Prose, 1966–1978* (New York: W. W. Norton, 1979), pp. 157–183.

AFTERWORD

1. Zora Neale Hurston, *Their Eyes Were Watching God* (New York: Lippincott, 1937).

2. John Langston Gwaltney, *Drylongso* (New York: Random House, 1981).

3. Gerda Lerner, ed., *Black Women in White America* (New York: Random House, 1973).

4. Barbara Christian, *Black Women Novelists: The Development of a Tradition, 1892–1976* (Westport, CT: Greenwood Press, 1980).

5. *Conditions: Five, the Black Women's Issue* (1979).

6. Toni Cade Bambara, ed., *The Black Woman: An Anthology* (New York: New American Library, 1970).

7. Mary Helen Washington, ed., *Black-Eyed Susans: Classic Stories by and about Black Women* (New York: Anchor, 1975).

8. Barbara Smith, *Toward a Black Feminist Criticism* (New York: Out & Out Books, 1977).

9. Chrystos, "No Rock Scorns Me as Whore," in *This Bridge Called My Back: Writings by Radical Women of Color*, ed. Cherrie Moraga and Gloria Anzaldua (Watertown, MA: Persephone Press, 1981), p. 243.

10. Octavia Butler, *Pattern-Master* (New York: Doubleday, 1976); *Mind of My Mind* (New York: Doubleday, 1977); *Kindred* (New York: Doubleday, 1979); *Wild Seed* (New York: Doubleday, 1970).

11. Jewelle Gomez, "No Day Too Long," in *Lesbian Fiction*, ed. Elly Bulkin (Watertown, MA: Persephone Press, 1981), pp. 219–225.

12. Gloria Anzaldua, "La Prieta," in *This Bridge*, ed. Moraga and Anzaldua, p. 204.

13. Audre Lorde, "The Beginning," in *Lesbian Fiction*, ed. Bulkin, p. 263.

14. Linda Hogan, "Sophie," in *Conditions: Seven* (1981), p. 14.

15. Pat Suncircle, "A Day's Growth," in *Lesbian Fiction*, ed. Bulkin, p. 4.

16. Hattie Gossett, "billie lives! billie lives!" in *This Bridge*, ed. Moraga and Anzaldua, pp. 108–111.

17. Rosario Morales, "I Am What I Am," in *This Bridge*, ed. Moraga and Anzaldua, p. 14.

18. Cited by Ora Williams, Thelma Williams, Dora Wilson, and Ramona Matthewson, in "American Black Women Composers: Selected Annotated Bibliography," in *All the Women Are White, All the Blacks Are Men, but Some of Us Are Brave: Black Women's Studies*, ed. Gloria T Hull, Patricia Bell Scott, and Barbara Smith (Old Westbury, NY: Feminist Press, 1982), p. 298.

19. Nellie Wong, "Grandmothers," in *Conditions: Four* (1979), p. 54.

20. Kitty Tsui, "Poa Poa Is Living Breathing Light," in *Lesbian Fiction*, ed. Bulkin, p. 174.

21. Alice Walker, "In Search of Our Mothers' Gardens: The Creativity of Black Women in the South," *Ms.* (1974), p. 105.

22. Cherrie Moraga, "La Guera," in *This Bridge*, ed. Moraga and Anzaldua, p. 27.

23. Cherrie Moraga, "Anatomy Lesson," in *Conditions: Seven* (1981), p. 8.

24. Jo Carrillo, "Maria Littlebear," in *Lesbian Fiction*, ed. Bulkin, p. 19.

25. Maxine Hong Kingston, *The Woman Warrior: Memoirs of a Childhood Among Ghosts* (New York: Alfred A. Knopf, 1975), p. 24.

26. Paule Marshall, "Shaping the World of My Art," *Women's Studies Quarterly* 9, no. 4 (Winter 1981): 23–24.

27. Barbara Smith and Beverly Smith, "Across the Kitchen Table, a Sister-Sister Dialogue: Homophobia in the Black Community," in *This Bridge*, ed. Moraga and Anzaldua, p. 124.

28. Kitchen Table: Women of Color Press, Box 592, Van Brunt Station, Brooklyn, NY 11215.

29. June Jordan, "Getting Down to Get Over, Dedicated to My Mother," in *Keeping the Faith: Writings by Contemporary Black American Women*, ed. Pat Crutchfield Exum (New York: Fawcett, 1974), p. 105.

30. Flying Clouds, biographical note, in *Lesbian Fiction*, ed. Bulkin, p. 288.

Index